Forward

HISTORIC SITES ARE SPECIAL MUSEUMS that
accurately as possible the historical appearance and cha
us understand how people lived, worked, played, worshiped, or
Since 1958 the Mackinac Island State Park Commission has dev
historic site systems in the nation, telling stories of life at the Str
historic times to the present. Fort Mackinac, Historic Mill Cree
downtown buildings, and Colonial Michilimackinac all represen
tory of Northern Michigan and the Upper Great Lakes.

Visitors to these historic sites enthusiastically question and ex
story of how people were fed. From gardens at Michilimackina
at Mill Creek, to Victorian banquets and Army Commissary far
ries of food are of interest to almost every visitor and are import
life was lived.

With this book, Mackinac State Historic Parks shares with sit
of what we have learned about colonial period food preparation
mackinac frontier outpost. The recipes reveal patterns of season
which governed women's lives, and some of the tasks of men an
ping, gardening, trade, butchering, canning, cooking, baking, a
pear in this volume with historical details, and with recipes whic
today's kitchen. We invite you to explore *History from the Hear*
then by visiting the Mackinac State Historic Parks.

Carl R. Nold
Director
Mackinac Island State Park Commission

History
from the
Hearth

A Colonial Michilimackinac Cookbook

by

Sally Eustice

HISTORY
from the
HEARTH

A Colonial Michilimackinac

by Sally Eustice

Mackinac State Historic Parks
Mackinac Island, Michigan
© 1997 Mackinac State Historic Par

ISBN: 911872-67-1

First Edition
first printing: 5,000 copies

Editor: David Armour
Assistant Editor: Karen McCarthy
Art Director: Thomas Kachadurian

Photography by Thomas Kachaduria

TABLE OF CONTENTS

PREFACE

"Did the voyageurs really eat bear grease and dried corn for dinner?"

"What are those dried things hanging over the fireplace?"

"Roast beaver and muskrat stew? That's GROSS!"

"Didn't they get sick eating that stuff?"

"How did the women preserve food for the winters?"

"What foods did the settlers get from the Indians?"

"Did you really bake that bread under the ashes? How can you tell when it's done?"

"What kinds of fresh foods were available?"

"Do you folks really eat that stuff?"

These are the common, everyday questions and comments that summer visitors make as they wander into the reconstructed homes at Colonial Michilimackinac and visit with the interpreters. Here they meet the craft demonstrators who are preparing meals using traditional foods and methods of cooking.

As visitors walk along the shoreline to the fort they may find one of the Chippewa women making corn soup or the Ottawa man cleaning some fish. As they enter through the water gate they may see one of the women gathering fresh herbs to put in a stew or a soldier hoeing the carrots and corn. Guests often smell the aroma of onions and meat stewing or bread baking and come looking for the source. Upon entering the houses, they may find an interpreter preparing, serving, eating, or cleaning up. After a meal, visitors may follow one of the women out to the animal pens to feed the scraps to the chickens or help her gather eggs for the next meal.

Why do we recreate these colonial foodways? The procuring of foods and staples was essential to the existence of the early inhabitants. By researching some of the foods, we can learn a great deal about the transportation and travel of those times. By studying the methods of food preparation, we discover many of the common cultural practices of the era. We learn about the intermixing of the Indian, French, and British cultures and how daily life changed and evolved as new peoples came into the Straits of Mackinac area.

Many changes in subsistence patterns came about as transportation became more dependable and less work-intensive. The daily diet affected the health and welfare of every community member. The lack of sufficient foodstuffs was a constant concern, and much of the daily life of the inhabitants was involved in the procuring, preparing, and preserving of edible goods.

While working at Colonial Michilimackinac as a craft demonstrator, I became interested in learning more about the food preparation methods of the time. This book is a result of that search for information. Since there are no known written cookbooks from the fort in existence, information had to be gleaned from a variety of sources. Fortunately, there are many diary accounts of travelers, explorers, missionaries, and traders who lived in or passed through the area. These include accounts by Alexander Henry, John Porteous, Jesuit missionaries, administrators like Cadillac, and traders such as John Askin. John Askin left a large number of papers, including inventories of his household goods, which greatly help in determining what furnishings and utensils were available for use.

Some of the traders at the fort were Indians from the area, so we include foods of their culture, particularly from the Ottawa and Chippewa tribes.

During the 1770s British soldiers garrisoned the fort, bringing the influence of their foodways. We are able to recreate typical soldier fare of the British period by consulting the many surviving military records.

Other sources include facsimile reproductions of cookbooks from these periods, as well as research from other historic sites portraying the same time. Dr. Keith Widder, Curator of History, has assembled a craft interpretive manual, which has been supplemented by other staff members through the years. This collection of recipes, materials, and historical documentation has proved an invaluable resource.

Archaeology reports from this site have provided much information. Under the direction of Dr. Donald Heldman and Dr. Lynn Morand, archeology students and volunteers have dug, screened, preserved, and catalogued thousands of artifacts left by early residents. They dig up large numbers of food remains, especially bones, as well as objects used in food preparation. Through painstaking research they are able to identify seed types, bone fragments, and other remains, even differentiating between the French and British eras.

This book is arranged in two sections. The first part deals with the history of the area as it pertains to the culture and food habits of the people who resided in or traveled through Michilimackinac. The second section deals with documentation of foodstuffs and gives some examples of how foods were prepared. A few adaptations to modern times were made in the interest of health and safety and because some of the ingredients are no longer obtainable in the same form as in the 1770s.

This book is dedicated to the many friends and coworkers who encouraged its progress, especially:

Dr. David Armour, Deputy Director of the Park, who first said, "We ought to have a cookbook for the visitors," and then took my rough draft and turned it into a real book.

Dr. Keith Widder, Curator of History, who said "Why not make it a foodways book? Take what we know and flesh it out a bit."

Phil Porter, Curator of Interpretation, who just kept asking, "How's the book coming?"

Dr. Don Heldman, Dr. Elizabeth Scott, and Dr. Lynn Morand, who direct the staff archaeologists, and who gave us facts and research.

Lewis, who said, "You really need to trade that typewriter in on a computer," and then showed me how to use it!

Katie, who started the fort food program, and baked that first loaf of bread!

Lucy, who continued and built up the program, and who taught me to use cast iron pans.

Mary, friend and coworker, who shared her 12 years' experience in working in the craft program.

The many summer college students and workers who tried out these recipes, including Barb, Teri, Joanne, Cara, Alisa, Carol, Gretchen, Heidi, Leigh Anne, and all those who came before.

Jim and Keith, who supplied all that muskrat, beaver, and venison, and who never complained about stacking and splitting cords of wood.

Larry, Tim, Mike, Adam, Mark, Greg, Lew, Jeremy, Dan, and countless others, who taste-tested all these foods and spoke words of encouragement.

Barb, master gardener, who challenges us to produce our own garden vegetables.

Librarians everywhere—especially Mackinac and Petoskey—with their wonderful Michigan collections, and Joyce in Cheboygan who just kept smiling and saying, "Sure, I can order another list on interlibrary loan for you!"

The reenactors who shared their recipes, book sources, and enthusiasm for 18th-century life.

The visitors who kept asking "Why?" "How do you?" and "Could you send a copy of that recipe?"

And finally, to my many elementary students who kept saying, "Ms. Eustice, if we have to write a report, then you should, too!"

FOOD ON THE FRONTIER

WHO WERE THE PEOPLE who lived at Michilimackinac? What was their daily life like? What
hardships did they face? How was their life similar to or different from ours? How did they spend their day? It is difficult
for interpreters to give good, clear answers to these questions
asked by visitors. If we could travel back in time and live
among the Indians, French, and British who resided here,
then we could give a better answer. Since that's not possible,
we look to their words, searching history for understanding.

The study of food helps us learn a lot about people. Nourishment is a common need of all classes, ages, genders, and
groups. The ways in which food was obtained, cooked,
served, and talked about by the people of the straits area in
the 18th century tells us a good deal about who they were.
Sometimes food was simply a matter of nourishment to
them; other times it became a social event. During times of
famine, it was a matter of life and death. At times of feast, it
was a part of the celebration. Even their religious life was re-
flected in their diet, as they avoided certain foods in fasting.
The economy of the area often revolved around obtaining
food and selling it to others. There are stories from those
who procured the food: the hunters, farmers, and fishermen
who lived at the straits.

Most of the travelers who passed through Mackinac made
observations on the foods available. They wrote home and
told of the harsh winters, the abundance of fish, and the mo-
notony of corn. They corresponded with others and ordered
goods from the East. The military officers kept track of the
goods in the storehouse and made sure their men had flour
and salt pork. The traders recorded transactions for corn and
rum and supplies for the North country. On occasion, they

ordered special items such as cheese and fine wines. Others recorded the planting of potatoes, peas, and beans. Altogether, these written words from the past tell us a story of the ordinary life of an 18th-century Mackinac inhabitant.

One of the biggest difficulties in preparing this book was the lack of written records left by women. There is no known recipe book or diary from a woman who lived here. Therefore, recipes from other places during this time are used to show the methods of cookery. Most of the recipes in the following chapters are generalized, based on the foodstuffs we know were available and what was customary at the time.

The first people in the straits area were native people who hunted, fished, and raised corn. The Huron were here in the 1600s and the Ottawa and Ojibwa had villages here in the 1700s. Other tribes passed through as they traveled the waters of the Great Lakes to the east and west. The geography of the straits area at Mackinac formed natural stopping places for anyone traveling by canoe. This remains so as we gather to cross the Mackinac Bridge between Michigan's peninsulas.

The Huron Indians built a village on the north side of the straits, where St. Ignace is located today. They had been pushed out of their ancestral homes, further east, by the Iroquois Confederacy. Father Pierre Marquette, a famous Jesuit missionary, also built a chapel and mission at this site. Later, the French constructed a small military post, Fort du Buade, to monitor the fur trade. The missionaries wrote about the abundance of whitefish and the corn raised by the Huron.

Antoine Lamothe Cadillac, the French officer in charge of Fort du Buade at St. Ignace, set his sights on a better opportunity to develop a settlement at Detroit. He convinced the government to abandon the straits post in 1701 and to grant him land at Detroit. Without the military in the area, the excesses of the rum and fur trade became difficult for the missionaries to cope with. They decided to leave Michilimackinac.

Mackinac was abandoned by the French until 1715, when

they erected a small outpost on the south side of the straits, at today's Mackinaw City. This fort was enlarged several times. The Jesuits established a church, St. Anne's, on the site. The Ottawa built a permanent summer village nearby, at L'Arbre Croche (Cross Village). They were encouraged to do so by the French, who wanted them settled nearby.

The natives supplied the French with large amounts of corn, upon which both the traders and the military depended. The French Commandant of Michilimackinac, Sieur de Celoron, did everything he could to aid and encourage the Ottawa to remain nearby. He even wrote the Governor General of New France telling how he sent soldiers to help the Indians prepare the soil for planting in 1741.[1]

About ten French families as well as the French soldiers lived year-round at the site. During the summers the fort was the hub of the fur trade. Here merchants brought supplies from Montreal to exchange for the furs the traders gathered from the West. During each short summer season a great deal of business was transacted, and then things quieted down for the winter months. Most people returned to their homes in the East or left for their winter posts. Even the Ottawa moved south toward the Grand River, where less snow made for better hunting during the winter. The French relied on trade to supply their food rather than producing it themselves.

A French military engineer, Lotbinière, visited the fort in 1749. He drew maps and left a written description of what he observed. His map is especially important because it labels houses with the names of the people who lived in them. The map labels a building outside the fort as "*écurie à Mr Langlade*" or the stable of Langlade. Also located outside the fort walls are two bake ovens, labeled "*fours.*" Along the right side of the "*place,*" or parade ground, is a garden which adjoins the court of the Jesuits. A small door in the fort's west wall gives access to an enclosed area where there is a "*glacière*" or ice house, and a "*four,*" or bake oven.

Turlington's Balsam of Life bottle

Fort Michilimackinac was much more than a military outpost. It was also a centrally located, fortified fur trade post. The military served as the government in the region. The commanding officer controlled the fur trade licenses and dealt with the native peoples. The palisaded fort served as a collection and storage depot for the furs and trade goods, which were sent both east and west when the seasons permitted.

The French presence in the area expanded as trade increased. Settlements at the Sault and Detroit were important to those who lived at Mackinac, and travel was common between these sites. Mackinac became especially important during the French and Indian wars. No battles were fought here, but the French and Indians from the region traveled south and east to fight in many battles. Charles Langlade, for example, led men in the defeat of General Braddock at Fort Duquesne, served under Montcalm at the siege of Fort George (William Henry), and was on the Plains of Abraham at Quebec in 1759. Langlade returned to Michilimackinac and was placed in command of the post by Louis de Beaujeu until the British arrived in 1761.

The first British trader to come to Mackinac was Alexander Henry. He was there to welcome the arrival of the British soldiers who came from Detroit in 1761. Henry was in the fort on the King's Birthday, 1763, when the Chippewa surprised the fort and killed or captured all the British. Inspired by Chief Pontiac, forts all over the Midwest were captured. Henry was rescued by his Ottawa friend, Chief Wawatam. Henry's memoirs, written later, provide great insight into daily life at Michilimackinac.

In the summer of 1766 Lieutenant

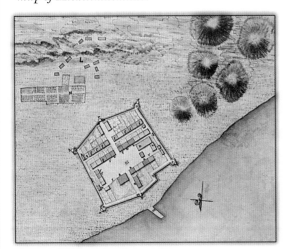

Perkins Magra's 1766 map of Michilimackinac.

Perkins Magra drew a map of Michilimackinac for the British command. His map included stables and fenced gardens outside the fort walls, as well as gardens within the stockade. The stables were located where the animals are kept in today's reconstructed fort. The gardens were located outside and to the left of the land gate. The map shows ten sections of a garden, enclosed with a pole fence. The fence would have been an aid in keeping the rabbits out—a problem we have at Mackinac today! We have planted a heritage apple orchard near this spot, as there is a reference to apples planted "near the old garden gate." The map also locates small gardens behind many of the traders' houses, within the walls of the fort.

Trade increased under the British. A Scots-Irish trader, John Askin, left many written records. Askin had a farm about three miles from the fort and he kept a garden diary for two years. He also kept a household inventory for several years; these lists are used to help determine how to furnish the houses. He corresponded with business partners in Detroit, Albany, and Montreal. He had several sailing ships that traveled between Detroit and Mackinac, including the sloop *Welcome*. The *Welcome* Logbook, kept by Captain Alexander Harrow, records the comings and goings of the 45-ton sloop.

Askin married Archange Barthe, from a prominent Detroit French family, and they raised nine children, plus three he had had with an Indian woman. These children married, went into business, and traveled. Some of the letters they wrote home are published in the John Askin Papers. Askin was very prominent at Detroit, after he left Mackinac, and knew all the leading men of his time. His papers provide information about family life at Mackinac as he writes of his daughter's wedding, orders shoes for his wife, and tries to figure out how to keep his family fed and his business profitable. Askin's letters often included short messages from his wife to some of their mutual acquaintances. On one occasion Askin wrote to Mrs. Charboillez, concerning some business he contracted with her husband. While Mr. Charboillez was in the Lake Superior country, his wife was doing his business correspondence and making sure of supplies.

British officers left many records as they corresponded to their superiors back East. They requisitioned supplies, sought permission to enlarge and eventually move the fort, and sent reports of what was happening in the area. A considerable amount of correspondence concerns the difficulty in getting adequate food supplies to Mackinac during 1778-79. The Americans were in revolt and shipping was difficult. Supplies were needed in the East and Mackinac was at the end of the supply line. Askin's ships were confiscated by Captain Arent Schuyler De Peyster in order to transport military supplies. Askin continued to seek ways to get his corn, rum, and other supplies to Mackinac, so he could fulfill his commitments to the traders in the North.

De Peyster was replaced by Patrick Sinclair in 1779. Sinclair immediately began to negotiate to move the military to Mackinac Island. In fact, he started preparations before gaining General Haldimand's approval. Sinclair did not get along well with John Askin, who decided to leave and return to Detroit. The fort at Michilimackinac was eventually abandoned, in favor of a better position on Mackinac Island. The French civilians, under the Treaty of Paris, had been allowed to retain their property within the walls of the British fort. This made the British officers uneasy. They were also concerned about the lack of a proper harbor for their sailing ships, as the beach in front of the fort was shallow and rocky and really only suitable for canoes. The wooden walls of the fort, surrounded by fields and forest, were not adequate for protection from a feared American attack. Therefore, the British began to build on the bluff of the island, moving buildings and belongings by ship and over the ice in the winter. The church was moved and located below the fort. The walls and buildings from Michilimackinac were torn down and the wood reused on the island. The civilians there settled in a town, under the protection of the fort walls. The Indians camped along the beaches of the island when they came for their treaty payments. The remains of the old fort were burned down and the site abandoned in favor of the new Fort Mackinac.

The site remained abandoned, used as a park and campsite by summer visitors, until its reconstruction was begun in 1959. An active archaeology program, a lively summer interpretation program, and museum displays now complement the reconstructed site. Part of the interpretation includes the foods and crafts program, the focus of this study. Visitors love to help in the gardens and watch food being prepared in the fireplaces. They want to know more of this frontier life and how it worked. It has taken many hours to collect and organize this material to help interpret the civilian life at Michilimackinac. We hope it will be a help to everyone interested in 18th-century life at a fur trade post. As more information is discovered by historians, archaeologists, and history buffs, the fort's program continues to change and improve.

This creamware plate and many other artifacts excavated at Michilimackinac are on display in the underground exhibit, Treasures from the Sand.

18th-Century Cooking Methods

THIS CHAPTER IS BASED on 18th-century cookbooks and practical experience learned while cooking in the fireplace at Michilimackinac. One of the most common questions visitors ask is "Where did you learn to cook like that?" When I tell them I was a home economics major in college they just smile, and we laugh about the changes that have come about in the last 200 years. When I reflect back, though, I recall the final project I presented in my college "Teaching of Home Economics" class. I led my classmates outside, where we built a campfire next to the parking lot. I then demonstrated how to make biscuits using a reflector oven, how to cook eggs and bacon over an open fire in a paper sack, and how to plank a whitefish! Twenty years later I found a place (Colonial Michilimackinac) where they would let me do things like that all day and even pay me to do it!

The nostalgia and romance of a nice roaring fire and a log home prompt many of us to want to return to that lifestyle. It's fun, but you'll also learn to appreciate your gas or electric stove, your refrigerator, and especially running water! The first requirement for an 18th-century woman must have been the ability to lift tremendous weights. The fireplace requires constant refilling, the cast iron kettles can weigh up to 40 pounds, and the yoke, with two full buckets of water, is a real back-breaker. Barrels of flour weighed 196 pounds and firkins of butter weighed 56 pounds. The refrigerator was either a root cellar, a snowbank in winter, or an ice house. She might have to saw a roast off a frozen carcass hanging in the ice house. There were no canning jars, plastic wrap, or instant mixes. The nearest food warehouse was in Detroit, so they had to plan well, purchase supplies by the barrel, and lay up lots of extras for the winter. If you are willing to give up con venience in exchange for good, basic food, then this might be for you!

The fireplaces in wilderness outposts like Mackinac were very basic. They were small, with an open hearth and perhaps a crane. There were no draft or damper systems back then. When it rained the water came right down the chimney. When the wind came off the lakeshore the smoke drew forward, into the house, rather than up the chimney. Most of the heat goes up the chimney. We learned, during the winter openings at Colonial Michilimackinac, that boiling dishwater can freeze in twenty minutes, less than ten feet from the fireplace. A family would probably have had the blacksmith make and install a crane. Several pots can be suspended from these, and they make it easier to add wood to the fire. Every hearth needed some kind of andirons. These are metal stands that hold the logs up off the stone floor of the fireplace. They had a front bar which kept the burning logs from rolling out into the house.

Accidental fire was a concern, as sparks could shoot out onto a wood floor. A woman's skirts could drag in the embers and catch on fire. A chimney fire could ignite and burn the whole house down. Burning ash could ascend up the chimney, land on the cedar bark roof, and start the whole roof burning. Perhaps one of the biggest dangers was tipping over a scalding hot pan of water or soup. Dutch ovens were placed on the hearth and hot embers placed under, over, and around them. There had to be a constant awareness of the power of fire, flame, and hot kettles. The fireplace is very inviting, and on a cold winter day the family would all sit near it. The extra congestion and traffic by the cook's stove must have made things difficult.

The type of wood used in the fireplace is very important. The most essential requirement is that it be dry. Any logs over 5 inches in diameter need to be split. Our Native American interpreter taught us a valuable lesson in fire starting. He always collects any scraps of birchbark left from building lodges and uses these to start the blaze. In a race with paper, birch bark wins every time. We also have a good, dry supply of cedar kindling. This makes a fast, hot flame and is better than any barbecue starter fluid. We never clean out all the ashes, as these are needed to create a draft. Just clean out the area under the andirons, build a small blaze with bark and kindling, and then add on a few split logs. The best wood for baking is hardwood. We prefer beech, oak, and maple. (The guys who split the wood prefer the beech and oak—never elm, which they claim is the hardest to chop!) These hardwoods produce the hottest and longest-lasting coals.

It takes at least 30 minutes to get enough coals to get started. We do put a kettle of water on right away, as we need hot water for making bread, doing dishes, or cleaning up just about anything. If you plan to do any serious bread or pie baking, then load the fireplace full and get as many hot coals as possible. An 18th-century cook probably never let her fire go out, as the family could add to it all evening and even during the night. Since we leave the fort when the park closes, we let the fires go out in the late afternoon.

A simple soup or stew can be prepared by hanging a kettle on the crane and simmering or boiling some water, meat, and vegetables. If the kettle is open, this allows the cook easy access for stirring. However, a lot of evaporation occurs and some of the flavor is lost. We often use open kettles at the fort because visitors want to see the food, not a pan lid. A good compromise is to leave it open while adding ingredients and working with it, but then cover it up and slide it to the side to cook slowly, to develop its full flavor and tenderness. A kettle hung on a crane acts the same as a burner on a stove. What you get is hot heat, applied to the bottom of a pan.

A small stone fireplace acts almost the same as an oven with the door open. A lot of heat reflects off the back and side walls, as well as the heat that is produced by the flame.

Fires were started by striking a piece of flint stone with an iron "strike-a-light." The sparks fell on a piece of tinder and were blown into a flame.

An efficient cook utilizes all her cooking space by placing water kettles beside the andirons and by heaping coals on the stone hearth. If you want to use a griddle or fry pan, then shovel a layer of hot embers out onto the hearth. Cover this with a layer of old ashes, which helps retain the heat and prevents hot spots. Place a trivet over this. Three-legged trivets are best as they are easiest to level. Place your griddle or pan on the trivet and proceed with flipping your pancakes or frying your salt pork. You will need to replenish the coals about every 20 minutes. Make sure you have some spatulas and forks with very long handles. This is where it's easy to singe all the hair off your arm!

Dutch ovens can also be placed on the hearth, in a pile of coals. Some people prefer to use a trivet with them, but I prefer to have them really buried down in the coals. Dutch ovens can be used to roast a chicken, bake a pie, or steam a pudding. We will examine each of these methods separately.

To roast a ham, turkey, or chunk of venison, just place it in the pan, set it in the coals, cover, and let it bake. Check occasionally and add more coals, if necessary. I like to add enough water to baste, or at least to keep it from burning on the bottom. A domed lid is good, as it fits best over a plump turkey or ham. There is no need to cover the lid with coals—they just might get into the food. This bakes like an oven set at about 350°. If you are cooking a greasy cut of meat, like a goose, duck, or mutton, then set the meat on a low trivet placed inside the Dutch oven. This will keep the meat from sitting in its own fat.

To bake a pie in a Dutch oven, place the oven in the ashes to preheat. Place a trivet in the bottom of the oven. Prepare the pie in a pie tin and just set the tin in the oven. Cover with the lid and heap coals on top. For this, use a lid with a lip edge. This keeps the coals from rolling into the pan when you check your pie. Cakes can also be prepared this way. Just pour the batter into a cake tin, place it in the oven, and bake. Another way to bake a cake is to pour the batter directly into the pregreased oven, cover, and bake. This works well unless the batter has a lot of sugar or fruit, which might burn to the bottom.

Another way to use a Dutch oven is to steam a pudding in it. A rice pudding, custard, or Boston brown bread can be put in a crock or oven-proof bowl, and set on a shallow rack with an inch or two of water in the bottom of the oven. Cover tightly with the lid and let it bake slowly. This is especially good for foods that burn easily, such as milk and cheese.

The last method we use is simply hanging meat over the fire and turning it slowly, like a rotisserie. We hang Cornish hens (in place of passenger pigeons) from a string attached to the crane. If you spin them clockwise, they will slowly untwist and expose all sides of the meat to the heat. Some andirons had racks for spits attached to the front. Other spits were freestanding. I prefer these, as you can place a tin underneath to catch the juices, and you can adjust the heat by adding more coals where you need them. This method requires close attention or the meat can dry out quickly. We like to hang venison ribs, on an "s" hook, from the crane and let the fat melt off, into the fire. When most of the grease is gone, we put the ribs in a pan, cover with sauce, and bake until tender.

Tin reflector ovens were in use during our time period, but we haven't found reference to their use at Michilimackinac and therefore choose not to use them. Our fireplace hearths are really too narrow to accommodate them safely anyway. We do know that serious bread baking was done in outdoor bake ovens. We even know that there were two bake ovens located just outside the land gate. These were usually built away from houses, to prevent the chance of accidental

OPPOSITE PAGE: *Colonial Michilimackinac is open daily from mid-May to mid-October. Costumed interpreters bring Michilimackinac to life. The smell of gunpowder blends with the odors of savory meals cooking in the fireplaces and over outdoor fires. Sounds of gunfire mingle with the bleat of sheep and the fiddle music of a wedding dance.*

fire. Perhaps someday these will be reconstructed and we'll have a chance to bake in them.

We do occasionally build an outdoor fire for projects like soap making, food drying, and cooking up a bushel of apples into apple butter. Fire safety, windy weather, and the close monitoring this requires limit how often we can do this. This doesn't mean it should limit you from trying it. In fact, if you don't have a fireplace, you could try most any of these recipes outdoors. Many a summer visitor has watched a meal prepared in the fireplace and then gone back to their campground and baked a pie or loaf of bread! Try it, you'll like it.

We need to address the issue of whether or not you should wash your cast iron and how you should season it. When you first purchase your pan, it will come with a layer of oil to prevent rust. This must be washed off! After you've cleaned it, heat your pan in a fireplace or oven, or on a barbecue grill. Wipe it with a layer of solid vegetable shortening. We have found vegetable oil will leave a very sticky residue. Let the shortening melt and bake in. Recoat and reheat, until the pot darkens. The first few times the pan is used you should plan to fry or cook greasy foods, as this will add to the coating. Try never to scrub your pan hard enough to remove this coating or you will have to reseason it.

We only wash the pans when they had meat, wet foods like soup, or burnt-on sugar. If you bake a bread or cake, simply tip the food out, wipe out the bottom with a paper towel, and wipe another layer of vegetable shortening on. If you do this while the pan is still hot, that's all you have to do! If the pan is cool, then place it back in the fire and heat until the grease is melted in. If it is necessary to wash the pan, try to just pour hot water (without soap) in it, and wipe out with a spatula or wooden spoon. Try not to scrape the seasoning off. Washed pans must go back in the fireplace or oven to dry out or they will be rusty the next time you want to use them. Always, always, always, put them away dry and greased!

Modern Methods

These recipes can easily be adapted to gas or electric stoves. The source of the heat doesn't matter when you are boiling, simmering or stewing. Just use your own experience and sense of time to adjust temperature and length of cooking time. A crock pot or slow cooker can also be used to prepare these wet foods. Keep in mind a modern stove will provide a more consistent temperature than a wood fire which by its nature cools down until more fuel is added.

We grow heritage vegetables in our gardens at Michilimackinac. For sources on heritage seeds see page 209.

The pies and cakes can be baked in your home oven as well as a Dutch oven. The wood fire usually produces a temperature between 325° and 375°. Just place your pie tin or cake pan in your regular oven and check it often. You can also place cast iron kettles on a stove top or in an oven as well as in a fireplace.

Most of the bread, cake, and pie recipes give a time and temperature setting. When we prepared and tested these recipes at Colonial Michilimackinac they were all done in the fireplace. Also, we used them to demonstrate to the public and often had the lids off to show the people what was cooking. When prepared at home, they may cook a little faster, as there is less need to check the food.

When we prepare these foods at Michilimackinac we try to think like an 18th-century cook and use what they had. We use vegetables and fruits in season. We use lots of wild game and fish and some beef. They must have often substituted one meat or vegetable for another and we encourage you to do the same. We adapt to the weather. When it is humid the bread rises faster and when it is freezing out it takes longer to roast a turkey. If extra people come for dinner we thin the stew to a soup or add potatoes to make the meat go farther. We don't measure seasonings but rather taste to see if it's right!

Fireplace cooking is forgiving. It just smells and tastes better when it takes a little longer to make. Your family will wait till it's done and may think it's so good they'll do the dishes!

18th-Century Cookbooks

The foods we cook at Michilimackinac are based on ingredients that we know were available at Mackinac. Written records and archaeological artifacts tell us what they used. From this point, we have to look elsewhere to see how foods would have been prepared. There were few cookbooks available in America at this time; most women prepared recipes from memory or their own handwritten receipt books. Several of these early cookbooks and receipt books have been republished. Professional food historians have researched many facets of American foodways and made their work available. Other historical sites of our time period have also done research and published cookbooks. A journal, "Food History News," is published quarterly with contributors from many historic sites. Finally, there is the Association for Living Historical Farms and Agricultural Museums (ALHFAM), which holds national conferences where people from the various historical sites get together and share knowledge.

A number of recipes are based on these sources.

The Art of Cookery Made Plain and Easy, Hannah Glasse, first printed in London 1745, revised 1796. Facsimile editions printed by United States Historical Research Service, Schenectady, New York, 1994.

Martha Washington's Book of Cookery & A Book of Sweetmeats, Manuscript 1749-99, reprinted 1981 by Columbia University Press, New York, edited by Karen Hess.

The Compleat Housewife, E. Smith, 1753, reprinted 1968 by Literary Services and Production, England.

Mrs Gardiner's Receipts from 1763, Anne Gardiner, Boston Mass., reprinted 1938 by White & Horne Co.

The Frugal Colonial Housewife, Susannah Carter, 1772, reprinted 1976 by Doubleday.

The First American Cookbook 1796, Amelia Simmon, facsimile

reprinted 1958 by Oxford University Press and 1984 by
Dover. First cookbook authored by an American and
published in the United States.

Thomas Jefferson's Cookbook, written by Martha Jefferson
Randolph's daughter, Virginia, and compiled, reedited
and added to by the Jefferson Foundation, University
Press of Virginia, 1976.

Seventy-five Receipts for Pastry, Cakes and Sweetmeats, Eliza
Leslie, 1828, republished by Applewood Books,

The American Frugal Housewife, Mrs. Child, Boston 1833,
reprinted by Applewood Books.

*Peter Kalm's Travels In North America, The English Version
of 1770*, edited by Adolph Benson, reprinted 1987 by
Dover.

Peter Kalm is much quoted in this book. He was a Swedish naturalist who traveled throughout New York, Pennsylvania, and Canada in 1749 and 1750, leaving wonderful
descriptions of plant and animal life. He was also very obser-
vant of social customs and repeatedly tells about the common
ways they do things in America. He describes many foods in
great detail and tells how the British, French, and Indians
treated each of these foods. Although he never reached
Mackinac, he lived and traveled in all the places in the East
which our traders and soldiers came from.

As you read the following chapters you will find primary
source quotes from people who lived at Mackinac in the 18th
century. These will be supplemented with a little general history and background, when needed to flesh out the story.
There will be lots of hints on general fireplace cooking. Finally, there will be a generalized recipe for using these foods. This
is "how we really cook it at Michilimackinac." Try them, and
next time you're in the straits area, please stop by and let us
know if you like 18th-century cooking!

SOUPS

ONE-POT DISHES such as soups and stews were standard daily meals. This was the plain, everyday cooking, which would give the cook time to complete other household chores as well. Many cooks were limited by their cooking equipment and may only have had one or two pots to cook in. Other times there wasn't much variety in raw materials or groceries, and they just put what they had together and heated it up. Another of the major reasons for cooking one-pot meals was rediscovered by Michilimackinac staff at our winter openings. Several weekends during January and February the fort is opened for special events. As we prepared meals in the fireplaces, we discovered many problems not encountered in the warmer, summer season. The water froze in buckets, within a few feet of the fireplace. When boiling dishwater was poured into a brass dish pan, a layer of ice formed on top before the dishes were done. When the wet dishes were set on a wood table until they could be dried, they froze to the table. The problems of washing up several cooking kettles and serving and eating dishes in the wintertime would certainly encourage the use of simple meals!

A big advantage in using a single soup pot is that it requires less fuel. When an iron pot is hung from the crane, the bottom is centered over the fire and heated from the warm air going up the chimney. When a Dutch oven bakes on the hearth, coals are raked out and surround the pot. In the wintertime these coals cool down so rapidly that it requires much more firewood to cook this way. We also found people tended to crowd close to the fires in January. If there were many kettles, with hot ashes on the hearth,

Heavy cast iron pots, an essential part of any household, were used for heating water or cooking soup.

Tips for making soup in fireplaces, learned by experience:

1. *Place the soup kettle on the crane in a position that when swung out, it will not hit the andirons, tip, and spill soup over the fire you just built.*

2. *Start water to boiling early. It takes a good supply of coals to produce much heat.*

3. *For a thick soup or stew, dredge the meat in flour first, brown, and then proceed with your recipe. It will be self-thickening and won't need additional cornstarch or flour.*

4. *If you don't have a crane and your kettle is sitting in the coals, make sure it is covered when adding more wood or moving equipment around. It's really annoying to have a log land in your kettle!*

5. *Add more liquid if your kettle starts to go dry. Scraping out burnt food takes all the nice, seasoned coatings off pans and you'd really rather be doing something else anyway.*

continued on page 29

this would increase the danger of fires and burns and leave less room for warming up cold hands and feet.

It was pretty common to keep a pot of soup on the crane and add more meat or vegetables from the root cellar as needed. As the soup cooks, it thickens to a stew. If it boils dry it becomes a hash. If too dry it becomes ash. A cook could make the food go farther by adding more water and thinning out the stew and making it soup! Most of the soup and stew recipes have the same ingredients and the only difference is how much liquid is in the kettle.

General soup advice from period cookbooks tells the cook to add the meat to cold water. If more water is needed because of evaporation, add boiling water, as cold water will spoil it. To have a clear broth, the scum and grease had to be skimmed off. It was suggested to throw in a little salt to bring up the scum. Most recipes said to simmer, not to let it boil hard. The pot should be kept covered so the flavor would not cook away. Because we are cooking foods as a demonstration at Michilimackinac we often have the lids off the pots to show visitors. This has led us to the obvious discovery of another very good purpose of lids for wet foods. The covers keep fireplace ash and cinders out of the soup pot!

If you choose to make these soups on a conventional gas or electric stove, just place the ingredients in a heavy soup pot and proceed with the recipe. The cooking times should be very similar. You could also prepare these in a crock pot.

FISH

Fish were particularly abundant at Mackinac during certain seasons of the year. They could be counted on at least to supplement the salt pork and corn of the early residents. Native Americans came to the straits, where they established seasonal fishing villages and gathered large numbers of lake trout, white fish, and sturgeon. When the first Jesuit missionaries came, they built a mission near one of these Huron villages, at present-day St. Ignace. Joseph Marest, a Jesuit priest, wrote from there, saying:

"This spot is the most noted, in all these regions for its abundance of fish, since in Savage parlance, this is its native country. No other place, however it may abound in fish, is properly its abode, which is only in the neighborhood of Missilimakinac . . . In fact, besides the fish common to all the other Nations, as the herring, carp, pike, golden fish, white-fish, and sturgeon, there are here found three kinds of trout; one, the common kind; the second, larger, being three feet in length and one in width; and the third, monstrous, for no other word expresses it,—being moreover so fat that the Savages, who delight in grease, have difficulty in eating it. Now they are so abundant that one man will pierce with his javelin as many as 40 or 50 under the ice, in three hours' time."[1]

BOUILLABAISSE
Fish Soup

2 lbs	fish, gutted and scaled
¼ lb	bacon or salt pork, cut in cubes
2 sm	onions, chopped
4	carrots, chopped
4	potatoes, peeled and cubed
	salt and white pepper
	water

Cut the fish into chunks. Historically, the bones and head were included and then strained out afterward—it's much easier to filet the fish first. Cut up and fry the salt pork. Add fish, cover with water, and stew until tender. Add vegetables and simmer until tender. You can substitute turnips, celery, or any chopped vegetable. Season as desired. Serve hot.

6. *If you are adding milk or cream, don't put the pan back in the fire. There is enough resid-ual heat in the warm pan and food to heat it. Milk products will scorch or burn quickly.*

7. *Fresh garden peas added to your soup will turn the broth a very unusual shade of black in just a few minutes.*

8. *Don't place a cast iron kettle of soup on the table unless it's on a trivet. It will decorate your tabletop with nice round burn rings. We leave it on the hearth or woodbox and serve from there.*

Use any type of fish—carp, perch, whitefish, cod. We have lots of pike in this area but don't use that in fish soup because the Y-bones are too difficult to remove and they cause serious choking problems.

It's always a good idea to serve bread with fish soup. If someone swallows a bone they should eat bread to push it down!

A similar soup is the fish chowder, below. It has the same ingredients, with the addition of milk and cream. Milk would have been available at Michilimackinac in the spring and summer months but not during the winter. "Milch" cows were fed mainly harvested meadow grass. This grass was cut in Cheboygan and then rafted or loaded on Askin's ship, *Welcome*, and brought to Mackinac. With this kind of diet, cows dried up and did not produce milk during the winter. They would "freshen" in the spring, when they had calves, and then produce milk for the summer.

Fish Chowder

¼ lb	salt pork, cut in cubes
2 lg	onions, chopped
3 lg	potatoes, peeled and cubed
2 cups	water
2 tsp	salt
2 lbs	fresh fish, cut in small chunks and boned
2 cups	milk
2 cups	light cream
3 T	butter or margarine
	pepper to taste

Brown salt pork in a soup kettle, until all fat melts out and cubes of pork are crisp. In another kettle, boil onions in water for 10 minutes. Add potatoes and salt, cover, and simmer 20 minutes. Put potatoes, onions, and water into the kettle with the salt pork. Add boned fish, cover, and simmer until fish is done and breaks apart. Add milk, cream, butter, and pepper. Heat 5 minutes. Serve hot with sippets of bread. Sippets are slices of bread, buttered and toasted, often cut into triangles.

Chicken

Chicken Soup

	chicken	1	onion
½ tsp	salt		pepper
	water	3 T	fresh parsley

Place ingredients in an iron soup kettle and hang on a fireplace crane. Bring to a boil and let it simmer about an hour. Remove the chicken, let cool, and pick the meat off the bones. Discard bones and return chicken pieces to pot. Add other ingredients as desired and/or available (½ cup brown rice, barley, wild rice, or homemade noodles). Add parsley just before serving.

VARIATION: Make a cream soup by adding a white sauce made from 1 T butter, 2 T flour and 1 cup milk.

Cock-a-Leekie Soup
Chicken-onion

1	stew hen	1	onion
10	peppercorns	1	bay leaf
1 T	salt		water
6 sm	leeks, white part (substitute a bunch of wild leeks, if available)		
¼ cup	raw rice (white or brown)		

Place stew hen in a large pan and cover with cold water. Add salt, peppercorns, bay leaf, and onion.

Bring to a boil, skim, and then simmer until chicken is tender, about 2 hours.

Remove the bird. Strain the broth, removing onion and bay leaf. Add leeks, sliced thin. Add rice. Simmer until leeks

Askin inventory, 1776:
- *20 Fowles*
- *24 Fowels* [2]

are tender and rice is done. Add 1 cup chopped chicken meat. Serve the rest of the meat separately.

MEAT

Askin diary,
February 24, 1775:

The Ewes began to Lamb.[3]

Slight mention is made of lamb or mutton at Mackinac in the 18th century. This reference Askin made is tucked between references to cows and pigs. This, and his inventories which list a "pair of Sheep Sheeres, 2 Crooks at the farm, and 1 pair of Wool Cards" are the only primary sources documenting sheep located so far. The inclusion of the wool cards and sheep shears leads one to believe the sheep were more important for their wool than for their meat. However, elsewhere in the country, sheep were used as meat, mainly because of their size. When an animal was butchered, especially in warm weather, the meat had to be used immediately or be salted and dried. A sheep was small enough for a family to use within a few days. It seems reasonable that Askin, with his Scots-Irish background, would have introduced sheep to the area. A 1779 census of Detroit lists 313 sheep, 664 horses, 1,076 hogs, 1,811 cows and oxen.[4] Askin regularly sent his sloop *Welcome* between Detroit and Mackinac and probably brought the sheep from there.

MUTTON BROTH

Based on a recipe found in Thomas Jefferson's 1800 Cookbook [5]

1 lb	mutton neck bones	½ cup	barley
1	onion, chopped	1 cup	chopped, carrots
3	turnips, sliced	2 stalks	celery, chopped

Place mutton neck bones in a soup pot and cover with water. Bring to a boil, skimming off the foam. Add barley and simmer for 2 hours. Add carrots, turnips, celery, and onion. Simmer 2 more hours. Lift out meat with slotted spoon. Remove meat
from bones and return meat to pot. Season to taste and serve.

OXEN

An ox is a older steer or cow that has been trained as a draft animal. They were used to pull wagons and plows. When they reached the end of a useful life, they were butchered and used for meat. The meat would be tough and stringy, not the well marbled beef we see in the grocery store today. To be tender, the meat needed long, slow cooking with lots of liquid. A special meal was prepared from the tail. This part contains a lot of cartilage and makes a nice, thick gel-like broth.

Alexander Henry, 1762:

The Jesuit missionary killed an ox which he sold by the quarter, taking the weight of the meat in beaver skin. [6]

OXTAIL SOUP OR STEW
If it's thin, it's soup. If it's thick, it's stew!

1	package oxtails	1 lg	onion, sliced
3 cups	water	1 T	dry parsley
6-8	peppercorns	1 lg	bay leaf
	carrots, turnips, leeks as desired		
	Seasoned flour		

Brown oxtails in seasoned flour. Set aside and use the pan to fry onion until golden brown. Return oxtails to pot. Add parsley, peppercorns, and bay leaf. Add water, turnips, leeks, and carrots.

Cover and cook 1¼ hours.

BEEF

Fresh beef was available at Michilimackinac. Cows are too big to bring in a canoe so they must have been herded to Mackinac from Detroit along one of the old Indian trails. Today's I-75 highway traces an old trail. This trail was described as 18 inches wide and leading through bogs and swamps.[7]

A former French Michilimackinac officer, Repentigny, was granted a tract of land where today's Soo Locks at Sault Ste. Marie are located. In the winter of 1752 he wrote to a superior, La Jonquière, and said "I bought a bull, two bullocks, three cows, two heifers, one horse and a mare from Missilimackina."[8] These animals were probably walked across the frozen Straits of Mackinac to reach the Sault. They were likely used as draft animals to clear the lands and haul logs. At some point, when they were no longer fit to work, they might have been butchered and utilized for this recipe.

POT AU FEU

3 lbs	short ribs
1 T	salt
2	carrots, sliced
1 stalk	celery
2	turnips, peeled and sliced
1	parsnip, peeled and sliced
2	onions, studded with cloves
1	whole clove of garlic
1 bunch	wild leeks or green onions
	water
	flour

The name of this French beef soup translates as "pot in the fire."

Flour ribs and brown slightly. Add all ingredients to a soup kettle, cover with water, and simmer for 5-6 hours. Remove onions and celery stalk. Serve warm with bread.

VEGETABLES

Although most corn was dried and made into hominy or cornmeal, there were a few weeks at the end of summer when fresh corn was available. There were some garden plots outside the land gate of the fort where large plants like corn could be produced to provide fresh food. The majority of the corn cultivated in northern Michigan was grown by the Ottawa at L'Arbre Croche, between the present-day Cross Village and Harbor Springs. Here the lake effect of Lake Michigan, the wind protection provided by the dunes, and the richer soil led to better crops than the barren area around the fort. This "Indian corn" was the corn the traders and military purchased to lye and dry for traveling food. Archaeology at Michilimackinac shows that it was generally "Eastern 8 row flint corn" that was grown in this area.

CORN SOUP

2 oz	salt pork or bacon	4 cups	fresh corn
1 lg	onion	1 lb	potatoes
2 cups	chicken stock	2 cups	milk
	salt and pepper		

Cook bacon. Save bacon grease and use to saute onion. Add corn, potatoes, chicken stock, and milk. Simmer till done, but do not allow to boil.

A modern cook may make this year-round by substituting frozen or canned corn.

PEASE

Dried pease were standard rations for British military. The private soldiers commonly pooled their rations and made a kettle of thick pea soup. This is an especially easy and cheap food to make when serving a lot of people. When we prepare a large meal for special events, we usually prepare a pot of pea soup, without ham, for those who prefer a vegetarian meal. If you want to prepare a large kettle for a noon meal, then either presoak the peas in a bowl of water all night, or start your soup at sunrise.

In 1748, a Swedish naturalist named Peter Kalm traveled throughout New England and Pennsylvania. He remarked, "in all parts of Canada which are inhabited by the French, the people sow great quantities of them (peas) and have a large crop." [9]

Some heritage seed sources state that it was the yellow pea that was grown in Canada. We have been using them in the French kitchens and they have proved quite entertaining. Most visitors have never seen yellow peas and are sure we are trying to pass off corn as peas. If you try this, make sure to save a handful of dried yellow peas to prove it is really pea soup. They are available in larger grocery stores, usually packaged in a box and sometimes in a gourmet section.

When interpreting foodways, it is fun, educational, and entertaining to tie in information about social customs and language. Youngsters often ask why the barrels in the King's Storehouse are labeled "Pease." We are able to explain that "Pease" is the plural spelling of pea. Through time the "silent e" was dropped. We then show them the wooden bowls we serve the soup in and explain they are called "treen" ware. "Treen" was the plural for tree, and these wooden bowls came from a tree. This can lead to a discussion of how early pioneers made the things they needed from the materials that were available to them. It also teaches how our language has evolved through the years.

PEASE SOUP

1 lb	dried, split peas
3 qts	water
2 lg	onions, chopped
1 cup	chopped carrot
1 slice	ham, cut in bite sized pieces
	herbs and seasonings (thyme, salt, pepper)

Combine all ingredients in a large kettle and bring to a boil. Reduce heat to very low and simmer gently. Remove the lid, after an hour, so the liquid will reduce somewhat. Stir occasionally to keep from sticking. There is nothing worse than trying to scrub out a cast iron kettle with burnt pea soup! Soup may be thinned with water or broth if it gets too thick. When it will support a spoon, straight up, your soup is done.

This soup also calls to mind the following rhyme. Old cookbooks from Great Britain give recipes for a "pease porridge pudding" which is included in the vegetable section of this book. Perhaps that is the cold version some prefer?

Pease Porridge hot
Pease Porridge cold
Pease Porridge in the pot
Nine days old.

Some like it hot
Some like it cold
Some like it in the pot
Nine days old.

**Askin diary,
April 29, 1774:**

*planted Onions for seed,
also Beans Squash seed &
Cucombers.*

May 28, 1774:

*Sowed Garden Pease,
Beans, Clover & rye
Grass* [10]

BEAN SOUP

1½ cups	dried beans, presoaked overnight
	ham or beef bone
6 cups	water
1 lg	carrot, chopped
1 med	onion, chopped
	salt
¼ tsp	pepper
1 T	chopped fresh parsley

Bring beans, meat, and water to a boil, cover, and simmer.
Add vegetables, stir, and cover. Cook 1 hour. Season with salt
and pepper. Garnish with parsley and serve with fresh bread.

**Askin diary,
Nov 30, 1774:**

*Took up my Cabage out of
my Garden* [11]

CABBAGE

Askin, a Scots-Irish trader and British commissary agent,
married Archange Barthe June 21, 1772. She was from a
prominent Detroit family, of French descent. Askin already
had 3 children from an Ottawa Indian woman. Archange
took those children into her home and she and John had 9
more. Their family is an example of a very "blended" family
—Indian, French, and English! The children wrote in French
and spent time with Archange's relatives in Detroit. They
married or went into business with the British, except for
Adelaide. She married Elijah Brush, an American lawyer, in
1802 in Detroit. Her oldest brother, John, led a group of
Ottawa and Chippewa against the Americans in the War of
1812 attack on Mackinac Island!

LA GARBURE
French Cabbage Soup

1	cabbage, quartered
$^1/_4$ lb	bacon or fresh salt pork
	leftover meat (pork, venison)
1	onion, sliced
1 cup	chopped carrots
3	potatoes, chopped
	seasonings

Cut cabbage in quarters. Scald it, squeeze out the water, roll up each quarter, and place in a kettle. Layer it with salt pork, venison or any leftover meat.

Add onion, carrots, and potatoes. Add a layer of bacon and cover with water. Simmer over low heat for at least 2 hours. Lay a slice of bread in a bowl, spoon a serving of meat and cabbage on top. Add a ladleful of broth and other vegetables. Serve warm.

ONIONS AND LEEKS

Garden references show that onions were grown at Mackinac. Wild leeks or wild onions also grow in the woods throughout the area. In the springtime the woods in the St. Ignace area are especially abundant with wild leeks. These would have been available and used. Wild leeks look like chives but smell and taste like very strong green onions or scallions. Much of the household advice of the time warned not to let the cows get into these wild onions or they would "sour the milk."

18th-century cookbooks show onions boiled and served as a vegetable, added to stews, roasted with meats, and used to season many foods. No reference was found to eating them raw. The French are famous for this soup.

Askin diary:

Tuesday May 2d, 1775 Sowed Persley, Beets, Onion, Lettice & Barley Seeds

Wensday May 3d Sowed More Garden Seeds & sett Shallots & beans [12]

ONION SOUP

6-8	onions, peeled and chopped
$\frac{1}{2}$ cup	butter
1 cup	flour
4 cups	water
2 cups	beef stock or bouillon
1 tsp	salt

Heat butter in a frying pan. Add onions and cook slowly until onions are transparent. Sprinkle flour over onions and stir often until they turn golden brown. Meanwhile heat water and beef stock in a soup kettle. Bring to a boil. When onions are cooked, add them to the liquid.

If desired, top soup with slices of dried bread and cheese. Cover until cheese melts. The cheese will lay on the bread. Serve hot.

BOUILLON

At Michilimackinac we cook a daily noon meal which costumed staff are served in a historic setting. We often make a pot of soup with one piece of chicken, or a whole kettle of stew with a small amount of meat. We use less expensive carrots and potatoes to fill up the pot. (We grow these right on site also.) To enhance the meat flavor, we add beef or chicken bouillon to the pot. After learning about "pocket soup" or "portable soup" we began to interpret how bouillon was a suitable food source to use. In fact, before the days of refrigeration, we suspect that many animal carcasses were used to produce this "dried soup" rather than being wasted. If the hunter didn't bring in fresh meat for the kettle, many a housewife probably cooked up some vegetables from the root cellar with a little of this instant soup mix!

Hannah Glasse, in a 1745 London cookbook, wrote

about making a dry bouillon mix. Broth was boiled down till it was a thick gel. It was placed in china cups and further cooked until it was like glue. It was then laid in the sun to further dehydrate. This dry soup was used later to make a broth or sauce.[13]

Mrs. Gardiner's recipe from 1763 told about pouring thick broth in a shallow saucer and letting it dry in the sun. It was then cut into shapes like coins and used to make broth later.[14]

If you wish to use bouillon in an historic setting, store cubes in a tin or glass container. It will draw moisture from the air and make a mess if just wrapped in paper or even stored in a wood box.

POTATOES

The soil around Mackinac is very sandy and actually quite good for potatoes. Because potatoes are underground, they are less susceptible to damage by windstorms and bad weather. We know potatoes were commonly grown here by the 1770s. Native Americans of this region used Jerusalem artichokes, which were commonly referred to as Indian potatoes.

CREAM OF POTATO SOUP

1 sm	onion, diced	1 cup	diced potatoes
1 cup	stock (bouillon)	3 cups	milk
	salt and pepper		celery seed
	fresh parsley		

Boil potatoes and onion in stock until tender. Add milk and seasonings. Garnish with fresh parsley.

Askin diary, 1775:

Thro bracking when Green, rotten Hay or any such Stuff on land where pease & Buck wheat have been, plow it in the Month of Sepr Harrow it in the Spring & Plant Potatoes with ye Plow without any more dunging.

When Potatoes are dug up in the fall Clover seeds may be sowed. [15]

**Askin diary,
May 18th 1774:**

*Sowed Squashes or
pumpkin Seed at the
farm* [16]

SQUASH AND PUMPKIN

Squash and pumpkin were commonly grown by Native Americans. They were planted in combination with corn and beans. The corn stalks grew tall and the beans climbed up them. The beans, a legume, absorbed nitrogen from the air and bound it to the soil. The corn used the nitrogen to grow strong and tall. The squash were planted between the corn rows and their big leaves helped shade out the weeds. Together these crops of corn, beans, and squash are known as the "Three Sisters."

Pumpkins and winter squashes were commonly stored in underground caches or root cellars. They would keep several months. Another way to preserve them was to cut them in thin strips and dry them in the sun. This dehydrated pumpkin could be used for soup, puddings, or pies.

SQUASH SOUP

1 clove	garlic	1 cup	chopped onion
1 stalk	celery, chopped	4 T	butter
3 cups	chicken stock	2 cups	heavy cream
2 cups	mashed, cooked squash (frozen works)		
2 T	fresh *or*	1 T	dried parsley
	salt and pepper		
	seasoning as desired		

Saute garlic, onion, and celery in 2 T of the butter. Place in a soup kettle with chicken stock, squash, and spices. Bring to a boil, then simmer for 10 minutes. Add remaining butter. Remove from heat and stir in cream and seasonings. Serve warm.

PUMPKIN SOUP

1 29-oz can	pumpkin	3 T	maple syrup
1/2 tsp	allspice	3-4 cups	chicken broth

Mix and heat until warm—use broth to thin as necessary. Garnish with chives and toasted pumpkin seeds.

SAGAMITY

Sagamity was a mainstay of the voyageurs' diet, from their earliest contact with Native Americans and throughout the years they traveled the Great Lakes by canoe. This dried corn was lightweight to carry and offered great food value for the space it took up in a canoe. With some "grease" and a kettle and perhaps a little dried meat or fish, the voyageur could cook up a filling meal at the end of a day of traveling. If he was lucky enough to catch some fish or game, that was tossed in the cookpot too! The dried corn was available throughout the Great Lakes region. It was grown by Native Americans and bartered to the French and British soldiers and especially traders. It appears to have been eaten by people in all class levels throughout Upper Canada and the Great Lakes region. Most times it was a main meal, but it was used as a side dish in banquets as well.

To interpret sagamity with today's foods, the easiest way is to purchase cornmeal ground as "grits" and located in the hot cereal section of the grocery store. Simply soak the cornmeal in some water and cook until it forms a thick porridge. Sweeten it with maple sugar, or add dried fruits or dried meats, if desired.

The earliest Jesuit missionaries traveling to North America mention sagamity as a common Native American food. This excerpt from The Jesuit Relations *describes what they first observed.*

. . . a Porridge made of the meal of Indian corn and water, morning and evening, and for a drink a flagon of water. Sometimes the savages put in pieces of cinders, to season the sagamité, at other times a handful of little water-flies, which are like the gnats of Provence; they esteem these highly, and make feast of them. The more prudent keep some fish after the fishing season, to break into the sagamité during the year; about half of a large carp is put in for fourteen persons, and the more tainted the fish is, the better. [17]

ACCOMPANIMENTS

Soups and stews seem more complete with crackers, noodles, or dumplings. If you would like to make your own, use these simple recipes.

DUMPLINGS

2 cups	flour	pinch of salt
½ cup	water	

Mix together until it forms a smooth paste. Drop by spoonfuls into boiling soup or stew. Cover and boil for 30-45 minutes. Resist the urge to peek, as the steam under the lid helps cook the tops of the dumplings.

HOMEMADE NOODLES

1 cup	sifted flour	½ tsp	salt
2	egg yolks	3-4 T	cold water

Sift flour and salt. Make a well in the center and add egg yolks and 2 T of the cold water. Beat with a wooden spoon until well mixed. Add 1 T water, mixing well with your hands. Dough will be stiff. Add more water if it is too stiff to knead. Knead about 5 minutes, until dough is smooth and elastic.

Divide into 2 parts. Roll out each part into a rectangle, noodle thickness. Roll dough loosely, as for a jelly roll. With a sharp knife, cut into strips for noodles. Unfold and place on a towel to dry. A dowel clothes rack also works well. Lay cheesecloth on top to keep the flies away. Noodles can be made ahead and stored in a glass jar. To use, add to boiling soup or stew. Simmer until done, about 8-10 minutes.

UNLEAVENED CRACKERS

2 cups	whole wheat flour	$^1/_2$ tsp	salt
2 T	dark brown sugar	dash	paprika
$^3/_4$ T	cold butter	$^3/_4$ cup	milk

Mix flour, sugar, salt, and paprika. Cut in butter to form a meal-like texture. Add milk and mix to a stiff dough. Cover and let rest 30 minutes. Preheat the oven.

Roll to $^1/_8$ inch thick. Cut into squares. Place on a cookie sheet. Bake at 375° until lightly browned.

ANOTHER CRACKER
With baking soda instead of sugar

4 cups	flour	$^1/_2$ tsp	baking soda
1 tsp	salt	$^3/_4$ cup	sour milk
1 cup	butter		

These would have been baked in an outdoor bake oven or perhaps a tin reflector oven.

Sift dry ingredients together well. Cut in milk and butter, making a stiff dough. Roll and turn until dough is very stiff. Roll very thin, cut into squares, prick with a fork, and bake at 375° until the edges are lightly browned.

Main Dishes

A BRITISH RHYME EFFECTIVELY describes the use of meat in the 18th century. When the hunter came in with a deer or the farmer butchered a pig, it had to be used as soon as possible, as there was no refrigeration. The cooks of the 18th century were experts at dealing with leftovers!

As the meat got older, more spices were added. By the end of the week it was the bones that were cooked for broth, and the small bits of leftovers that were added to potatoes to make them go farther. If the meat needed to be kept beyond this time, then it had to be salted, brined, soused (pickled), or dried.

Fresh meat at Michilimackinac was procured locally by hunters, raised by men like John Askin, or traded for with the Indians. In the 1770s most of the meat, at least for the military, was imported from the East Coast and even Europe. This meat was usually salted beef or pork. It was packed in wooden kegs and shipped, by canoe and later by sailing ships, along the water routes from Montreal and Albany. It often took many months for meat to reach Mackinac.

The earliest Europeans at Mackinac, the French voyageurs, seemed to be happy with their corn and "grease" with the addition of some fish. As the voyageurs traveled from Quebec and Montreal to Mackinac, they were known as *mangeurs de lard* or "pork eaters." They ate large amounts of fat, especially salt pork, to provide the energy to paddle canoes 14 hours a day. They had to be strong to portage the heavy bales of goods around the many waterfalls and rapids along the way. These same voyageurs brought supplies to Mackinac. Perhaps they were not as careful with someone else's food, as there were complaints that the meat arrived "rusty" and tainted. On a difficult portage, the voyageurs were known to pour off the heavy brine the meat was packed

Hot on Sunday,
Cold on Monday,
Hashed on Tuesday,
Minced on Wednesday,
Curried on Thursday,
Broth on Friday,
Cottage pie on Saturday.[1]

in. As they got closer to Mackinac, they filled the barrels up with fresh lake water. The meat would be inventoried and put away in the King's Storehouse and it could be several months before it was discovered that the meat was spoiled.

In 1778, the Michilimackinac British military garrison received 46,700 pounds of pork as well as 82,848 pounds of flour, 4,200 pounds of butter, 5,745 pounds of oatmeal, 544 bushels of peas, and 150 gallons of vinegar.[2] This was supplemented with fresh game and especially fresh fish, when available. Little meat, other than salt pork, was mentioned as being imported. The nearest urban market was in Detroit and only the more wealthy would have been able to afford it. It made more sense to raise a little fresh meat locally or to rely on hunting and fishing for free food. They had more time than money in those days!

There was a civilian population, as well as military, and they also had to acquire food. Askin said there were about 100 houses out in the suburbs that were "tolerably well built."[3] Some of these residents were only at Mackinac during the summer, but several families remained year round. These homes included French, English, and Métis (French/Indian) families and single men.

When meat supplies failed, residents could always fall back on fishing. Native Americans had come to this region for centuries for the abundant whitefish and lake trout. The French also depended greatly on the fishery. Many of them lived off the land as they wintered in the wilderness. The military sent men out to fish to supplement their salted and dried beef and pork. The British tended to hire some of the French to go fishing to provide extra supplies to feed some of the Indian visitors, to supplement rations for the private soldiers, and even to export back East to Fort Niagara. However, it seems the British had a preference for meat, when it was available. Some of the references to fishing, and how to prepare the catch, will be presented in the next chapter.

Following are many main dish recipes based on those of the 18th century. The wild game was used more often by the French and the salted and domestic meat by the British. However, both groups would have eaten whatever was available. The printed recipes of the time often included items, such as ocean fish and lemons, that were not available this far from the East Coast. The recipes below have been adjusted to include ingredients known to have been in the area. Fancy or time-consuming foods which would require a staff of servants to prepare have likewise been excluded. Many times, one meat must have been substituted for another. Probably the most common meat meal was some form of stew.

WILD GAME

BEAR

Native American people revered the bear. It provided them with warm furs and a very useful oil, as well as meat. There were many sacred ceremonies involved in bear hunting and the killing of a bear was not taken lightly.

Alexander Henry, a British trader at Michilimackinac, hunted bear with his Ottawa friend, Chief Wawatam. They dried the meat in front of a fire and the fat was melted down and stored in porcupine skins. This way the meat and fat could be transported when traveling by canoe or snowshoe.

If you are fortunate enough to have a hunter provide you with a piece of bear meat, consider it a treat. Clean it well, removing any bit of white fat. Marinate it all night in an onion soup broth. This will season it well. Drain the broth and either roast or stew the meat as you would a piece of beef. Serve it with potatoes and carrots. Use some beef bouillon, if you want gravy.

It was so difficult to get supplies to Mackinac that General Haldimand encouraged the post to use wild game as much as possible. He even offered to pay the soldiers the amount of money saved from rations!

BEAVER

The large number of beaver pelts that passed through the straits tells us that there was beaver meat available, at least at certain times of the year. Most beaver were caught or trapped elsewhere, and just their pelts made it to Mackinac. As the *hivernants*, or winter traders, left Mackinac for the northern and western regions, they relied much more on hunting to provide their sustenance. They would trap the beaver north of Lake Superior or as far west as the Mississippi. They would build a small post and trade with many different Native American groups. Since this meat was trapped in the winter, it could be frozen and used without salting or brining.

By the early 19th century the beaver population was in a decline and the beaver trade moved farther west. Because of the modern development of hunting laws with specific seasons, protection of wetlands, and less demand for furs, the population of beaver has again increased. In fact, there are many beaver in the Mackinac area today. They are sometimes considered a nuisance animal, as they cause a lot of damage to roads and drainage ditches. Our Native American interpreter spends much of his winter trapping and provides the kitchens with all the beaver meat we are willing to cook. Beaver tends to be a little more popular with the visitors who watch it being prepared, than with the staff who eat it for lunch! Our challenge has been to prepare and serve it to new staff members and ask them to tell us if they like it before learning what kind of meat it is.

Beaver is a very dark, red meat with a strong flavor. To prepare it, thaw the beaver in a bowl of water with cup of vinegar and 2 tablespoons of salt. This will draw off the blood. Beaver have several musk glands which must be removed or it will smell like skunk. Use a sharp knife to remove any white tissue, including all fat. Place the meat in a kettle of water, with a tablespoon of baking soda. Heat and skim off the foam as it cooks. If it is an old or large beaver, repeat with

This engraving from Middleton's Complete System of Geography *is titled "Beaver hunting in Canada."*

fresh water. You can do this the day before and refrigerate the meat, if you desire.

From this point the beaver may be treated like any other red meat. If it is a roast, set it on a trivet and bake in a Dutch oven. (Don't use the pan scrapings for gravy.) It is also ready to cut up and use as stew meat, which is what we usually do with it. Use lots of onions, turnips, potatoes, and rutabagas, and season with beef bouillon. Your guests will think you are serving beef.

FRIED BEAVER

Parboil **beaver** in a small amount of **water** until fork tender. Coat with **flour** and **seasonings** and fry in **shortening**.

ROAST BEAVER

Place **beaver** in a roasting pan. Cover with **sliced onions** and **bacon**. Add **salt and pepper**. Bake until tender. You may add potatoes, carrots, rutabagas, parsnips, or turnips to the roasting pan, or cook them separately.

BEAVER TAIL

Beaver tail proved to be a challenge to our staff. While the rest of the beaver is red meat, this is white. It looks like white gristle but is considered meat. Native American peoples considered this a treat. They used it as a source of fat, something that was hard for them to get in their diet. We tried to peel the skin off the raw meat but it refused to separate. We boiled one tail for 3 hours and still could not peel the skin off, although it thickened up like shoe leather. We tried slicing it and frying it but the skin was still too tough to cut. Finally, our Native American interpreter suggested we think like an Indian and use what they had. We just hung it over the fire and the heat on the hot fat caused the skin to split and peel back.

We decided it looked like salt pork so that's how we treat it. After it is peeled, cut it up and boil with a pot of beans. Add salt and pepper, and chopped onions.

FRIED BEAVER TAIL

Some recipes suggest dredging slices of tail meat in seasoned flour and frying till tender. Just remember not to serve it with tomato catsup. Tomatoes were considered poisonous in the 18th century and only used as garden ornamental plants. The catsups of the time were made of mushrooms and walnuts!

MUSKRAT

The taste of muskrat is very similar to beaver, and they are prepared the same way. Muskrats are much smaller, however, so it takes several "rats" to provide a meal. Most of the meat is in the legs and many people just prepare the drumstick and discard the rest of the animal. At Michilimackinac we usually make a stew with it.

The muskrat has several musk glands which must be removed before cooking. Usually this is done by the hunter as he skins and guts the animal. The cook, however, should carefully check the animal and remove any suspicious white or yellow tissue or her kitchen may smell like a skunk paid a visit!

If you want to prepare muskrat then you'll have to invest in a set of traps or find a friend who likes to run a trapline.

Soak **muskrat** in **salt water** with **2 T vinegar** for two hours. Drain. Put muskrat in a pan of **cold water** with **onion, salt, pepper,** and **celery.** Bring to a boil. When scum has formed, drain and rinse with cold water. Add more water and repeat this process until scum no longer forms. Continue

The muskrat is known by several different names—including "woods rat" and marsh rabbit. They are trapped mainly for their skin, but were also eaten as food. Some people are repelled by eating anything with the name "rat" attached to it. Others eat it to show how brave they are. Others relish the taste and the French in Monroe (near Detroit) even have a muskrat festival.

cooking until it has come to a steady boil. Drain.

At this point the meat may be treated several different ways:

1. Fry until meat is tender.

2. Put in a roaster, cover with cream style corn plus a little water, top with crumbs, cook at least 1 hour in the oven.

3. Roast in a cast iron kettle with vegetables and beef bouillon broth.

4. Cut the meat off the bones and use in a stew, with onions, potatoes, and carrots.

Rabbit Marinade

1	rabbit, cut up			
	vinegar		water	
1	whole onion	12	whole	cloves
1	bay leaf	1 clove	garlic	
1 T	salt	a few	peppercorns, bruised	
1 T	tarragon vinegar	1 pint	cream	
1/2 cup	flour		butter	

Cover rabbit in equal parts vinegar and water. Season with whole onion studded with cloves, bay leaf, garlic, tarragon vinegar, salt, and peppercorns.

Bring to a boil and then cool. Soak rabbit pieces in this brine for 24 hours.

Strain marinade and save it. Roll meat in flour and fry to a deep brown in butter. Pour in enough of the strained marinade to almost cover the rabbit. Cover the frying pan and simmer gently until the meat is tender. Remove meat to a hot platter. Reheat the pan juices, pour in cream, and stir vigorously until the sauce thickens. Pour sauce over meat and serve.

RABBIT PIE

8 slices	bacon or fresh salt pork
1	bay leaf
1 lb	mushrooms, sliced
3	leeks, chopped into 1-inch slices
1	rabbit, cut into small portions
	salt and pepper
3 T	parsley
3	potatoes, peeled and sliced
1 T	vinegar

Place bay leaf on the bottom of a Dutch oven. Layer with bacon, mushrooms, and leeks. Put rabbit in and cover with layers of remaining mushrooms and leeks. Add salt, pepper, and parsley. Put potatoes on top, sprinkle with salt, and add remaining bacon. Pour vinegar over the top. Cover and bake about 2 hours. Keep covered to retain juices. Serve warm.

This is much like a shepherd's pie except the potatoes are sliced rather than mashed.

RACCOON

Alexander Henry, 1764:

Raccoon hunting was my more particular and daily employ. I usually went out at the first dawn of day and seldom returned till sunset, or till I had laden myself with as many animals as I could carry.[4]

Raccoon is treated much like beaver and muskrat. It is skinned, the musk glands removed, and then dressed. It should be soaked in salt water overnight to draw the blood. Baking soda can be added to remove any gamey smell. It can be roasted, baked, stewed, or fricasseed.

RACCOON FRICASSEE

Cut coon into serving pieces and dredge in
seasoned flour. Brown in **hot fat**. Add:

1$^1/_2$ cups	water
$^1/_2$ cup	vinegar
1 med	onion, sliced into rings
1	bay leaf

Cover and simmer 2 hours until tender.
Thicken the juice with flour and water for
gravy. Serve hot with cornbread.

VENISON

VENISON PIE

1$^1/_2$ lbs	venison, cut in small cubes and browned
2 cups	water
$^1/_2$ tsp	salt
$^1/_4$ tsp	pepper
1	onion, coarsely chopped
1 T	flour
2 T	water
double	pie crust *(see page 84)*

Put venison in a pan. Cover with water. Add salt, pepper, and
onion; simmer until tender, about 30 minutes. Combine
flour and water; add this to the mixture in the saucepan.
Allow to cool. Line a pie pan with a pastry crust. Pour in
venison mixture. Put on top crust. Brush with butter and
make a slit for steam to escape. Bake at 350° for 1 hour, until
the top is brown.

Marinade for Jerky

Alexander Henry, 1764:

Wawatam killed a stag not far from our encampment. The next morning we moved our lodge to the carcass. At this station we remained two days, employed in drying the meat. The method was to cut it into slices of the thickness of a steak, and then hang it over the fire in the smoke. [5]

1 gal	water	$1/2$ cup	salt
1 cup	brown sugar	1 cup	molasses
$1/2$ tsp	ginger	$1/2$ tsp	nutmeg
$1/2$ tsp	ground cloves	1 tsp	onion powder
1 T	garlic powder	$1\ 1/4$ tsp	Tabasco
4 T	pepper	1 tsp	soy sauce
1 T	Worcestershire sauce	3-4 lbs	venison

Combine all the ingredients except the meat, boil 15 minutes, and stir. Let cool. Soak meat 1 hour. Drain. Dry meat on a Dutch oven trivet, hanging by the fire, or in the oven. This recipe is great for food dehydrators. They take about 12-16 hours to dry.

Venison Roast Marinade

1 cup	wine vinegar	2 cups	red wine
3 cups	cold water	1	onion, quartered
1 tsp	salt	8	whole cloves
1	bay leaf	1 tsp	dry mustard
1-3 lbs	venison roast		

Put marinade in a stone crock and immerse a roast in it. Weight it down so the roast is covered with liquid. Turn once a day.

Soak 2-3 days before roasting.

VENISON PASTY
Meat Pie

MEAT FILLING:

1 cup	venison, cooked and chopped		
1 med	onion, grated	1 sm	carrot, grated

DOUGH:

1½ cups	flour	⅜ cup	lard
½ t	salt	6T	water
	milk		

Mix flour and salt. Cut in lard until dough resembles coarse meal. Add water 1T at a time. Divide dough into 4 sections. Roll out dough; cut 4 circles the size of a tea saucer. Mix venison with onion and carrot. Add enough gravy (bouillon) to moisten. Season with salt and pepper. Divide filling between pastry rounds. Moisten the edges with water and fold over. Pinch edges together. Brush with milk. Bake 20-25 minutes, until brown.

VENISON MEAT LOAF

2 lbs	ground venison	2 tsp	salt
¼ tsp	pepper	¾ cup	milk
¾ cup	dry bread crumbs		
2	eggs, slightly beaten		
½ sm	onion, chopped		

Combine all ingredients and mix well. Bake at 350° for 2 hours. (Add salt pork if venison is dry.)

Venison Sausage

4 lbs	pork	8 lbs	venison
10 qts	potatoes	6	onions
1 cup	salt	1/3 cup	pepper
2 T	sugar		water

Grind pork and venison as for hamburger. Peel and grind potatoes and onions. Add salt, pepper, and sugar. Mix together and put in casings that have been soaked several hours or overnight. (Do this immediately or the potatoes will turn black.) Tie the ends and prick with a needle. Place in water, bring to boil, and simmer a few minutes. Cool. Wrap and place in the freezer.

When ready to eat, thaw and simmer about 10 minutes. Makes 35 rings.

Venison Ribs with Maple Syrup

3 lbs	venison ribs	1 cup	maple syrup
1 T	Worcestershire sauce	1 T	vinegar
1 sm	onion, finely chopped	14 tsp	dry mustard
1/4 tsp	salt	1/8 tsp	pepper

Hang ribs over the fire and let the fat drip off for 30 minutes. Cut into serving size pieces and place in a Dutch oven. Combine remaining ingredients in a separate pan and boil 5 minutes. Pour over ribs and bake, uncovered, for 1 hour. Baste, turn, and cook till done. Remove ribs to a serving dish. Skim the fat off the sauce and pour over the meat.

OPPOSITE PAGE: *Abandoned by British soldiers in 1781, the demolished fort was gradually covered by sand. Rediscovered by archaeologists in 1959, the fortified village is being brought back to life. Buildings are reconstructed on their exact sites as determined by careful archaeological excavations. Portions of the original 18th century buildings are preserved where possible. Many of the artifacts discovered by archaeologists are exhibited in the underground gallery,* Treasures from the Sand.

CORNED VENISON

20 lbs	venison	1 cup	brown sugar
2 T	salt peter	3 cups	coarse salt
4 cups	hot water		

Dissolve sugar and salt in water. Put in a crock. Add more water to cover venison by 2-3 inches. Weight it down. Cure 10-14 days. Rinse and put in a pot with:

1 T	thyme	2 T	salt
1 lg	onion, sliced	4	bay leaves
1 t	pepper		water to cover

Cook 3-4 hours, medium heat. Serve hot or cold.

    Corned meat was stored all winter in a barrel of brine. It would have to be below the frost line, in a root cellar, so it wouldn't freeze. Chunks of meat were removed and used as needed while the rest would remain in the brine.

Sinclair to Brehm, February 15, 1780:

Two Canadians are preparing Post & rail fence to enclose a fine grass Platt of about thirty acres for the King's Cattle which will be sent to the Island before the Ice breaks up. [7]

BEEF

The cows at Mackinac were probably the French-Canadian cow, descendants of stock brought to Canada from Brittany and Normandy. They closely resembled Guernseys. Adult cows ranged from 700-900 pounds and bulls up to 1,400.

    When a cow or ox was butchered, it would provide several hundred pounds of meat. Butchering time was traditionally in the fall, when the weather cooled. Fall butchering also meant that the cow would not have to be fed during the winter. A nice roast with Yorkshire pudding was probably served as a treat, but everything from the tongue to the "oxtail" would have been used. Even the hooves would be boiled down to make glue.

ROAST BEEF
WITH YORKSHIRE PUDDING

3-4 lbs   rib roast   **2 T**   oil

Coat beef with oil and roast, fat side up. Bake 1$\frac{1}{2}$ hours,
depending on how rare you like the beef.

YORKSHIRE PUDDING:

$\frac{3}{4}$ cup   flour   **$\frac{1}{2}$ tsp**   salt
$\frac{3}{4}$ cup   milk   **1 T**   water
2   eggs

Sift flour and salt into a bowl. Add milk and water gradually,
beating with a spoon. In a separate bowl, beat eggs until
fluffy. Add to flour mixture and beat until bubbles rise to the
surface. Cool for 1 hour.

　When the meat is cooked, remove from the pan and place
on a warm platter. Cover and let stand 25 minutes before
carving.

　Rebeat batter and pour it into still-warm cooking pan.
Bake it for 10 minutes at a high temperature. Reduce the
temperature (coals will cool naturally) and bake until risen
and golden brown, about 15 more minutes. Serve from the
pan in which it was cooked.

*John Askin
to James Sterling,
June 17, 1778:*

*I shall want a good Ox for
my own use between this
and the fall, the sooner you
can have him sent the better.* [6]

Red Flannel Hash

The beet juice will turn the potatoes pink, just like red flannel dye will run in the wash!

2 cups	corned beef, cooked and cubed
2 cups	potatoes, boiled and cubed
1 cup	beets, cooked and cubed
1	onion, chopped fine
3 T	butter or bacon drippings
1/4 cup	milk
	salt and pepper

Mix corned beef, potatoes, onion, and beets. Sprinkle with salt and pepper. Melt butter in a skillet. Add corned beef mixture. Pour in milk, adding more if the mixture is too dry. Flatten the hash into the pan. Cook over low heat until browned. Turn and brown the other side.

Corned Beef

3-4 lbs	corned beef	4	potatoes
6	carrots	1	onion
6	whole cloves	2 tsp	salt
1	head cabbage, cut in wedges		

Remove corned beef from bag and place it, along with any juices and spices from the package, in a kettle. Insert cloves into onion and add to the pot. Cover kettle and simmer 2 hours, until tender. Add carrots, potatoes, and salt about 1 hour before serving time. About 15 minutes before serving, add wedges of cabbage on top of meat and steam until tender.

Remove meat and let set a few minutes. Slice across the grain and arrange on a platter. Surround with vegetables, discarding onion. Serve the broth in a separate bowl to use as a thin gravy. Some folks like horseradish sauce with the meat.

During the winter the sailors and crew of Askin's sloop Welcome *were put to work cutting wood and building a cabin. On Thursday, March 16, 1776, this entry to the logbook was made.*

> *"No work done this day being held for St. Patrick's day"* [9]

Only one other holiday was named as a day off work and that was Christmas. Perhaps that crew fixed a corned beef dinner in honor of St. Patrick?

BOILED TONGUE

Beef (and buffalo) tongue were considered a favorite food in these times.

1	beef tongue
1	onion, peeled and sliced
1 cup	diced celery
1	carrot, peeled and sliced
1 tsp	salt
	peppercorns
	water

Cover tongue with boiling water. Add other ingredients and simmer until tender, about 2 hours. Drain, slice tongue in narrow strips, and serve hot or cold.

Michael Lotbinière, 1749:

At present, in the fort, there are 3 cows and one bull, 4 horses, one of which is a female mare, about 50 to 60 hens, 7 or 8 pigs. [8]

FORFAR BRIDIES

Individual Scottish meat pies

1 lb	minced, ground, or shaved beef
	salt and pepper
1/4 cup	minced suet
1	onion, minced

Mix meat with salt and pepper. Add suet and onion.

Make pastry dough (see page 84) and roll out small circles, 6 inches in diameter. Place filling on one half; fold and seal. Make a small cut to allow steam to escape. Place in a hot Dutch oven and bake about 30 minutes, until meat is done and crust is golden.

OPTIONAL: To make the meat go farther, or to save expense, you may want to add diced potatoes and rutabagas. Some prefer to have a beef gravy to accompany this meat pie.

This recipe is the equivalent of the "pastie" so common in the Upper Peninsula. Pasties were brought to the copper mining areas later in the 19th century by the Cornish miners who went to work there. Their recipes came from the British Isles, as did many of the "meat pie" traditions. The main difference between this early Scottish recipe and the traditional pastie of the Upper Peninsula is the use of rutabaga and potato in the latter.

PIRAGS
Meat-filled Pastry Turn-overs

Similar recipes show up throughout the British Isles. They had been common noon meals that could be taken along to eat on the job or while traveling. They stay warm if wrapped in cloth. Also, they are a great way to use up leftover stew or meat. Similar recipes, with a fish base, show up throughout Canada and in the Northwest.

PASTRY DOUGH:

¼ cup	lard	1 tsp	salt
2 T	sugar	2 cups	flour
1 pkg	yeast		
1 cup	hot, scalded milk		

Mix lard, salt, sugar, and milk; then add yeast and stir well. Add flour, turn out on a floured board, and knead, adding more flour as needed. Put dough into a greased bowl and let rise for 2 hours.

FILLING:

1 cup	chopped, raw bacon
¼ cup	chopped onion
	black pepper

Knead pastry dough again. Roll out to ¼ inch thick and cut circles with a biscuit cutter. Put a teaspoon of filling in the middle of each circle. Fold and pinch, sealing filling inside. Brush the tops with **egg** and place in a Dutch oven. Bake about 15 minutes, until crust is golden brown and shiny. Serve warm.

FORCEMEAT BALLS
Meat Balls

Many recipes call for "mincing" meat or chopping it very fine. This was a good use for odd cuts of meat. The cook controls the amount of fat in the ground meat by adjusting the amount of suet used. A cook could use a wood bowl and a "food chopper" which had a curved blade to mince the meat. She might also choose to pound it to a paste with a mortar and pestle. Modern food grinders and processors have sure made this task easier!

1 lb	ground veal or beef	1 T	minced onion
½ tsp	salt	dash	ground cloves
dash	pepper	1	egg
1 T	chopped fresh parsley		

Mix meat, onion, and spices in a small bowl. Add egg, mixing with your hands. Form mixture into balls 1 inch in diameter. Place in a hot, greased skillet and cook 30 minutes, until browned. Place in a bowl to serve. Plan on 3-4 per serving.

OPTIONAL: Some recipes called for a white sauce to be used as a gravy. This is good served with a dish of brown or wild rice. Other recipes call for a mixture of ground pork and ground beef, with sage as an extra seasoning.

Askin diary, 1775:

*March 4th
a Cow Calfed at the farm*

*March 25th
a Cow Calfed at the farm
in the Woods the Weather
so good & grass almost
Every place*

*April 1st
Some of my Cows have
lain Out for Near a
fortnight at difft times*

*Tusday [May] 9th
The Blk Cow & Mr
Morrisons Cow Calfed* [10]

MINCE AND TATTIES
Tatties are potatoes.

2 T	bacon fat or shortening
1 lg	onion, chopped
	minced beef (ground beef)
1 tsp	salt
1/2 tsp	pepper
1 handful	oatmeal
1/2 tsp	water or stock from boiling potatoes
1 lg	potato per serving

Melt fat, put in onion, and then add beef and brown quickly, stirring to prevent sticking. Add seasoning and oatmeal. Stir in water or stock and simmer 20 minutes. Serve with boiled or mashed potatoes. We ladle mashed potatoes in a bowl and top with this mixture.

SHEPHERD'S PIE

Combine:

	mashed potatoes		
1 T	grated onion	1	egg

Combine:

2 cups	chopped, cooked beef	2 T	butter
3 T	chopped parsley	1 tsp	salt
1/4 tsp	pepper	1/3 cup	hot milk

Place 1/2 of potato mixture in the bottom of a pie pan and cover with meat mixture. Top with remaining potatoes. Bake 25 minutes until browned.

OPTIONAL: Place grated cheese under the top layer of potatoes. If lacking enough leftover mashed potatoes you can place them just on top as a top crust.

STEAK AND KIDNEY PIE

FILLING:

1 lg	onion, chopped	6 T	butter	
1¼ lbs	cubed chunks of beef	½ lb	veal kidneys	
⅓ cup	flour	1 cup	mushrooms	
1 T	parsley		salt and pepper	
single	pie crust *(see page 84)*			

This recipe would have been very traditional with the British of the upper class.

Brown meat and onions. Combine with other ingredients and place in a pie shell. Cover with top crust. Bake until browned, about 30 minutes.

BASIC STEW

Roll **cubed meat** in **seasoned flour**. Brown the meat.

Cover with **water** and cook. Add **bouillon** if using a small amount of meat.

Add available vegetables—**carrots, onion, potatoes, turnips, green beans, corn, frozen peas,** etc. (Fresh peas will turn the sauce black!)

Cook till vegetables are tender. Thicken with cornstarch and water. **Salt** as needed.

April 8th
The red Sow piged had
Seven Pigs

April 12th
the poor white Sow had
one Pig

April 13th
The Black Sow Piged

Wensday May 3d
The small black Sow piged
& had six Pigs

Saturday the 6th
Capt Cornwalls Sow
pigged & had Eight Pigs

Nov 18th
The Black Sow Piged had
seven Pigs [11]

PORK

ROASTED SUCKLING PIG

A suckling pig, 6 weeks old, will weigh 12-15 lbs. Before cooking, the pig must be thoroughly washed. Remove the eyes and prop its jaw with a block of wood.

Stuff the pig with the following bread dressing.

1½ loaves	bread
4	onions, diced and simmered in butter
10	apples, diced
1 tsp	sage or poultry seasoning

Skewer or sew the opening shut. Place in a large pan, legs folded and tied into a kneeling position. Add cold water to the bottom of the pan to prevent scorching. Season with salt and butter. Encase the pig in buttered parchment or brown paper and bake 3-4 hours. (Until meat thermometer is 170°.) Baste with butter if skin becomes brittle. Cover ears and tail with foil if they begin to burn.

Place roasted pig on a platter. Replace the wood in its jaw with a red apple. Put grapes in the eye sockets. An herb garland can be arranged around its neck.

PORK SAUSAGE

2 lbs	lean pork, ground	1 cup	beef-kidney suet

Peel skin from suet and chop very fine. Combine with pork. Add desired **herbs and seasonings** such as sage, nutmeg, salt, and pepper. Let flavor develop for at least one week. To use, combine with **1 beaten egg** and **1 cup bread crumbs**. Make patties and fry or turn into casings.

Pork and Sauerkraut

2-3 lbs	smoked boneless pork butt
1 lb	bacon
2 qts	sauerkraut, drained
2	onions studded with 4 cloves each
	black peppercorns
2 cups	clear chicken broth (or bouillon and water)

Put meat in a large kettle. Place peppercorns in onion and place in kettle. Cover with sauerkraut. Add chicken broth. Bring to a boil and simmer, covered, for 1 -2 hours, until meat is tender. Discard onion. Place sauerkraut on a platter. Slice meat and arrange on platter. Serve warm.

Head Cheese

Soak the **head** and **hocks** in a **medium brine solution** overnight. Cover with **boiling water** and cook until the meat drops from the bones. Chop coarsely, place in a colander, and weight down to press out the fat. Cool the broth in a dish, allowing it to gel, and remove the fat. Season the meat with **salt, pepper, sage** and/or **other spices** to taste. Add enough gelled broth to make the mixture stick together and place in a tin pan to set. Slice and serve cold. (This is an early version of today's deli meats.)

Jellied Pig Hocks

Scrub **hocks** and soak in a **medium brine solution** overnight. Place in a large pot and cover with **boiling water**. Cook till tender. Remove skin and gristle. Take the meat off the bones and cut in large pieces. Season with **salt** and **pepper**. Place in a tin mold. Cook the broth and skim the fat. Pour over the meat to cover and let it set. Cut in slices and serve. (The broth sets up like today's unflavored gelatin!)

Michilimackinac, December 28, 1782:

By order of Captain Robertson Commandant we have survey'd one Thousand, one Hundred & twelve pounds of Flour, Five Hundred and twelve pounds of Pork, two Hundred Gallons of Pease, Five Hundred & Six pounds of oatmeal and twelve pounds of Butter, all of which we find unfit for human use, the Pork excepted which Tho' unfit for the use of His Majesty's Troops may be apply'd to the use of the Savages. [12]

Make brine from 1 gallon water and 1T salt. Pour off the brine the next day.

BOILED SALT PORK

2 lbs   salt pork
assorted vegetables as available (onions,
    potatoes, cabbage, carrots, turnips), chopped
salt and pepper
water

Freshen salt pork by soaking in a kettle of water at least two hours. If very salty, repeat soaking.

   Cut salt pork into chunks and brown in the bottom of a Dutch oven. Add water to cover and bring to a slow boil. Add vegetables and cook till tender. Season with salt and pepper.

SALT PORK WITH GRAVY

Slice a **slab of salt pork** into thin slices, like thick bacon. Fry until browned. Remove the meat from the pan and drain off all but 1 T of the melted fat. Pour in 1 **cup cream** and put the pan back over the heat. Scrape the pan with a spatula and continue stirring until the cream is heated through. Do not let it boil. Pour the sauce over the salt pork and serve warm.

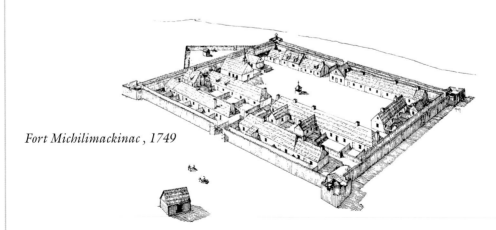

Fort Michilimackinac , 1749

Tourtière

French Canadian Pork Pie

This pork pie has become a Canadian tradition to serve at Christmas and is called *Tarte de Noël*. It is also served for Easter breakfast.

Filling:

1½ lbs	lean ground pork			
1	onion	2 T	butter	
1 clove	garlic, crushed	1¼ cups	boiling water	
1 cube	chicken bouillon	2 T	cornstarch	
¼ tsp	each: salt, pepper, sage, ground cinnamon, ground cloves			

Some recipes call for cinnamon and nutmeg. This sounds unusual in a meat pie but is delicious. Try it!

Brown meat and onion in butter. Add garlic, bouillon, and water and simmer 20 minutes. Add spices and cornstarch and stir throughly.

Meanwhile prepare pie crust:

2 cups	flour	1 tsp	salt
¼ cup	lard	6 T	water

Divide dough in halves. Roll out the bottom crust and place in a pie dish. Fill and add the top crust. Brush with beaten **egg yolk**.

Place pie plate in a Dutch oven and bake 1 hour or until crust is brown. This pie is often served chilled or at room temperature.

LAMB

LAMB STEW
Irish Stew

Askin diary,
February 24, 1775:

The Ewes began to lamb [13]

1 lb	lamb stew meat	4	onions, chopped
6	potatoes, peeled and sliced		
1 tsp	thyme	2 cups	water
	salt and pepper		

Remove excess fat and gristle from lamb and cut into cubes. Layer in a Dutch oven with potatoes, onions and seasoning. Top with a layer of potatoes. Add water. Place Dutch oven in coals and bake 2 hours. It is a good idea not to place coals on lids of wet foods like stew. They tend to fall into the stew while stirring and are difficult to remove.

ROAST LAMB
Purchase a fresh "spring" lamb and bake in a Dutch oven, just like a beef or pork roast. Older lambs are called mutton and they have a thick tallow fat that is not desirable. If using mutton, place it on a trivet and let the fat drain off. Don't use the fat for gravy as it has a low melting point and will turn to grease in your mouth. Lamb should be served warm. You may want to slice it and return it to the kettle. Leave the kettle in the coals and serve from the hearth.

Mint sauce is the traditional accompaniment for lamb. There is abundant mint growing along the lakeshore at Mackinac. We gather it fresh to make this sauce. Mint sauce purchased in today's grocery store is usually apple jelly with mint flavor. This recipe is tea-colored and does not have the artificial green dye used in today's canned mint jelly.

MINT SAUCE

1 cup	fresh mint, chopped fine
2 T	boiling water
2 T	sugar
4 T	white wine or white wine vinegar

Place mint in a bowl and pour boiling water over it. Wait 20 minutes while it forms a tea. Strain and add sugar and vinegar to the tea. Stir and serve in a gravy boat.

POULTRY

French settlers raised domestic chickens at Michilimackinac from very early on. Lotbinière, in 1749, listed 50 to 60 hens. Since chickens are the smallest and most portable of the domestic meats, they were brought in very early. They were probably placed in canoe crates and brought in by Jesuit missionaries from Detroit or Montreal.

A quick and easy way to roast a small fowl was to truss it up and suspend it over a fire with a twisted cord or string. This was called a "dangle spit." The cord could be twisted clockwise and then it would slowly untwist counterclockwise. A pan placed underneath could collect the juice to use for gravy. We use this method at Michilimackinac when preparing "pigeon" (Cornish game hens). The constant, close attention it requires would discourage the use of a bird that required 2 hours to roast!

Larger birds can be put on a spit and roasted, while turning by hand. A tin drip pan placed under the bird will collect the juices for gravy making. We place a little water in the pan so the dripping grease will not smoke and burn. Some andirons of this time period had brackets on the front to hold a spit. Other spits were freestanding. Some of the fancier homes in the big Eastern cities had special spit-turning

John Askin mentions chickens when he writes:

Jan 12th, 1775, the first hen laid Yesterday. [17]

Askin inventory, 1776:

24 Fowles @ 4/ for a total value of 4£ 16S.

1777:

2 Cocks & 6 Hens. [14]

1778:

20 fowels @ 8/ for a total value of 8£. [15]

1779:

31 fowles. [16]

devices called "clockjacks" but we have no reference to their use at Mackinac.

Another way we often cook a large turkey or goose is to place it in a large, covered Dutch oven and bake it. The finished bird looks like one baked in a roaster in a modern oven. This is the best method if you want to stuff the bird with dressing. It also means someone doesn't have to keep such a close eye on turning the spit. You need a 14" Dutch oven to accommodate a ten-pound turkey. A domed lid will fit better over a plump bird. If you use a flat lid refrain from putting coals on the lid. This will burn the skin before the bird is thoroughly cooked. The oven should be placed in a bed of coals and new coals should be added every 20-30 minutes. This will keep the temperature about 350°. We use the "shake the leg" test for doneness. When you shake the leg it should be very loose and the meat should be ready to fall off. If the skin starts to burn before the meat is done you can cover the drumsticks with tin foil (a modern method) or wrap a strip of bacon around it. The bacon grease will baste it and keep it moist.

A modern cook can simply put the bird in a roaster and bake until tender. It could also be prepared on a gas grill, using a barbecue spit.

CHICKEN GLACIES

1	stew hen	1	onion, whole
1 stalk	celery		

GLACIES:

1	egg, beaten	$^1\!/_2$ cup	milk
1 cup	flour	$^1\!/_2$ tsp	baking powder
dash	salt and pepper		

Cut up an old stew hen (one that no longer produces enough eggs to be worth the feed). Place chicken in a kettle of water with onion and celery. Bring to a boil and cook until tender.

When the chicken is nearly done, beat egg thoroughly in a mixing bowl. Pour in milk. Add salt and pepper. Gradually stir in baking powder and about 1 cup flour (enough to make the consistency of heavy cream). After the batter has been prepared, take the chicken out of the pan and bring the broth to a rolling boil. Tilt the mixing bowl of batter over the boiling broth and gently, but steadily, spoon out about 2 T of batter per stroke over the rim of the bowl into the broth. Cook in boiling broth 5-7 minutes or until firm. Spoon out and serve with the boiled chicken.[21]

CHICKEN STOVIES

Stovie is a Scottish term for "sweated" meat—it means meat cooked in moist heat. It should be cooked in a covered dish. The steam in the pan creates a moist, tender meal. A modern cook can make this easily in a crock pot.

1	chicken	6	potatoes
2	onions, sliced	2 T	butter
	salt and pepper		water

Boil chicken and cut the meat off the bones, saving the broth. Peel potatoes and cut up in slices. In a cast iron kettle, arrange layers of potatoes, onion, and chicken, sprinkling each layer with salt, pepper, and butter. Add broth to food surface and cover tightly. Simmer gently for 2-3 hours or until potatoes are tender. Add hot water, if necessary, to keep from burning.

APPLE STUFFING

Try this stuffing with your turkey or goose or duck.

$^1/_4$ cup	butter	$^1/_2$ cup	chopped onion
1 cup	chopped celery	$^1/_2$ cup	raisins
4 cups	pared, cored, chopped apples		
6 cups	bread cubes	1 tsp	salt
1 tsp	cinnamon	$^1/_4$ tsp	nutmeg

Saute onion and celery in hot butter until tender, about 5 minutes. In a large bowl, toss remaining ingredients until combined.

This will make enough to stuff a 10-12 lb turkey.

Bread Sauce for Poultry

This sauce is excellent when the birds are skinned, rather than plucked. With a fresh parsley garnish, the sauce covers up the bare meat. It can be served over boiled, baked, or roasted poultry.

2 whole	shallots, peeled		
1 cup	stale bread crumbs	2 cups	milk or cream
pinch	ground cloves	1 T	butter
	salt and pepper		

Combine milk, shallots, and crumbs and simmer 15 minutes. Discard shallots. Season with spices. Add butter and serve, poured over poultry.

This is also useful when game birds have been roasted on a spit and there are no juices to make a gravy.

Wildfowl

Wildfowl were hunted during the spring and fall migration periods. Some of the ducks were probably available through-out the summer. Domestic fowl were mostly eaten in the fall. A few "broody hens" and a rooster would be held over to start new eggs and chicks in the spring. The rest would be butchered so they would not have to be fed all winter. This fall butchering might have led to the British custom of serving goose on Michaelmas Day (September 29). This is the church feast of St. Michael, the Archangel. In the early 19th century, it also became traditional to serve a Christmas goose.

In April 1766 John Porteous wrote:

Went to the sugary upon the ice in the morning, having froze very hard last night, shot a pheasant 4 pidgeons & a Goose returned along the beach most part of the way on snow shoes 9 Miles the sun haveing made the ice too dangerous . . . April 25th, Little ice now in the Channel except some in shore driving into Lake Michigan some thunder, some pidgions now begin to cross the straits very high toweards the Gros Cape, the weather very cold & stormy. . . May 1st, Found but indifferent hunting, however kill'd a good many ducks, plover, Shaledrakes, teal, etc, thro' great labor & marching in water & marshes. [20]

ROAST GOOSE

Singe off any feathers. Wash **goose** inside and out with salt water. Stuff and place on a rack or trivet in a Dutch oven. Keep a little **water** in the bottom of the pan so the fat dripping from the goose won't smoke. Prick the skin with a fork so the grease can run to the bottom of the pan. Geese are very greasy and you do not want the grease to be absorbed by the stuffing. It helps to spoon out grease as the bird bakes. This goose fat should be saved for other uses. Use **butter** and/or **cider** to baste the goose. Roast 3-4 hours until done.

FRUIT STUFFING FOR GOOSE

3 cups	chopped bread	1/2 cup	butter
1 cup	chopped apples	1/2 cup	chopped nuts
1/2 cup	raisins	1/2 tsp	salt
1/4 tsp	pepper	1 T	lemon juice

Melt butter and pour over bread crumbs. Add other ingredients and toss lightly. Stuff the goose.

Some recipes included roasted chestnuts in the dressing. Others used chicken stock or applejack to moisten the bread. One recipe called for a pound of minced pork, 3 onions, and sage.

Dressing can also be made from cornbread. Leftover cornbread can be broken into crumbs and added to wheat bread crumbs. This can be combined with 1 onion, chopped and cooked in butter, 2 cups bouillon or broth, and seasonings.

WILDFOWL STUFFING

2 T	butter	$^3/_4$ cup	diced celery
$^1/_2$ cup	chopped onion	2 T	chopped parsley
1 tsp	salt	$^1/_4$ tsp	pepper
1 12-oz can	mushrooms	1 cup	cooked wild rice
2-3 slices	bacon		

Melt butter. Add celery, onion, and parsley. Add remaining ingredients and toss lightly. Spoon stuffing into cavity. Place on a shallow rack in a kettle. Place bacon slices over breast, which makes the fowl self-basting. Roast 2 hours.

PIGEON

Young pigeons are called squab. They are fat and tasty. Usually just the breast meat was used. The Chippewa boiled them with wild rice. They also impaled the plucked birds on a stick and roasted them before a fire. Pigeons were also used like other fowl, including chicken, duck, or goose.

Today's cook must substitute Cornish game hens or wild birds such as woodcock.

In the 18th century there were massive flocks of passenger pigeons. They migrated spring and fall between their wintering grounds and summer nesting areas. Some flocks flew along the Michigan shoreline and crossed the lakes at the straits where the Mackinac Bridge is today. These birds were caught in nets, clubbed in their nesting areas, or shot down. Passenger pigeons were hunted to extinction by the late 19th century. One of the last flocks sighted was on Mackinac Island in 1889.

PIGEON PIE

This recipe might remind you of the old English rhyme "4 and 20 blackbirds baked in a pie!"

4	pigeons (substitute Cornish hens)		
2	onions, sliced	2	carrots, sliced
1	bay leaf		peppercorns
4 T	melted butter	2 T	flour
	salt, pepper and tarragon to taste		
1 cup	cream (or evaporated milk)		
single	pie crust *(see page 84)*		

Truss pigeons and place in a kettle. Simmer 20 minutes with water, onions, carrots, and spices. Remove pigeons and strain the stock. Brown pigeons in melted butter in a skillet. Set into a deep pie plate. Add flour to the butter left in the pan and stir. Add 2 cups of strained stock and bring to a boil. Simmer 10 minutes, until thickened. Season as desired with salt, pepper, and tarragon. Stir in cream and heat through. Pour the sauce over the pigeons. Seal with a top pastry crust. Place in a Dutch oven and bake until crust is browned. Each person is served a whole, trussed pigeon with crust and gravy.

EGGS

The eggs used could have been chicken eggs, raised at Mackinac. As early as 1749, Charles Lotbinière said there were "50 or 60 chickens in the fort." If someone were lucky enough to find a nest of fresh wild duck, goose, or turtle eggs, they could have been used as well.

Eggs were not as available, year round, as they are today. Even chickens that were fed and kept in hen houses would not produce eggs during the times of year when there was not enough daylight. Eggs were as valuable as the meat produced by poultry. The eggs of many early breeds were brown-colored. Eggs of those days were small, so many recipe books called for large numbers of eggs when baking. Modern Grade A Large would have equaled two old-fashioned eggs.

French Catholics observed a 40-day fast during Lent. The day before Ash Wednesday (the beginning of Lent) was Mardi Gras, a day of feasting. They used up all the eggs and tasty foods before their fast began. During Lent, eggs were preserved until Easter. Eggs could be preserved by the following methods:

1. Have a barrel in the root cellar with a solution made of 2 gallons water, 1 pint coarse salt, and 1 pint of slacked lime. The eggs were added to this barrel as accumulated and they could be preserved for two years.
2. Coat the eggs with melted fat and pack in layers of oatmeal.
3. Rub the eggs with lard and pack in dry salt.
4. Scald the eggs in boiling water for one minute, cover with melted fat, and pack in powdered charcoal.

CREPES

Crepes are listed under main dishes, but they were also a dessert. They could even be considered a bread. Crepes were traditional with the French people from the 16th century on.

| 4 | eggs, beaten | 3 T | flour |
| ¹/₄ cup | milk or cream | pinch | salt and sugar |

Use a whisk to beat eggs. Add other ingredients. Heat a skillet and add **oil**. Pour a small amount of batter and rotate skillet to spread thinly. Cook like a pancake, browning both sides. Stack on a plate, keeping finished crepes covered and warm. Fill with fruit, jam, creamed vegetables, or seafood. Dust fruit crepes with powdered sugar. Maple syrup is also good, poured over the top.

One of our Mackinac favorites is to top the crepes with a white sauce that has bits of boiled whitefish in it. This makes a great main dish meal and is also a way to use up leftover fish. See recipe for Finnian Haddie, page 93.

PAIN PERDU
French Toast

This is French for "lost bread" and is a perfect way to use up stale bread before it molds.

2	eggs, well beaten	¹/₂ cup	milk or cream
dash	salt	8 slices	day old bread

Combine eggs, milk, and salt. Beat well. Place in a large flat bowl or pie tin. Dip slices of bread into the egg mixture and soak until well coated.

Heat a griddle and coat it with lard. Fry the bread slices on both sides until lightly browned and the egg is cooked.

Place on a plate and sprinkle with cinnamon and sugar, or add butter and maple syrup. Serve hot.

PANCAKES

English pancakes were traditionally served on Shrove Tuesday (the day before Ash Wednesday). Every household was supposed to use up all its eggs and milk before Lent began. This is similar to the French custom of crepes on Mardi Gras (Fat Tuesday).

1³/₄ cups	flour	pinch	salt
2 tsp	sugar	2	eggs
1	egg yolk	1 cup	milk
1 cup	water	3 tsp	melted butter
	sugar to sprinkle on top		

Sift flour with salt and sugar. Beat eggs and extra egg yolk and add to flour. Add milk and water and beat until the batter is frothy. Let stand 10 minutes.

Stir melted butter into batter. Heat oil on a griddle and cook the pancakes, flipping once. Pancakes should be very thin. Sprinkle with sugar and eat.

TARTE A L'OIGNON

Onion Quiche

This traditional Canadian recipe would be a good way to use up eggs and smells delicious when cooking.

Askin diary,
January 12th, 1775:

The first hen laid
Yesterday. [23]

6	onions, sliced		butter
3	eggs, beaten	1 cup	milk or cream
	salt and pepper		
single	pie crust *(see page 84)*		

Peel and slice onions. Fry in butter until golden brown. Beat eggs and milk together. Add seasoning. Stir in onions.

Line pie plate with dough. Add filling. Bake on a trivet in a Dutch oven until eggs are set.

Melt slices of cheese on top just before serving.

SCOTS EGGS

4	hard-boiled eggs	1 lb	pork sausage
1	raw egg	1 cup	bread crumbs
	salt and pepper and other seasonings to taste		

Peel hard-boiled eggs. Mix sausage and seasonings together. Dip hard-boiled egg in raw egg. Wrap with seasoned sausage mixture. Roll in egg again and then in bread crumbs.

Fry for 10 minutes, or until sausage is thoroughly cooked. Turn carefully, or meat will fall off! Delicious served with pancakes and syrup.

This recipe is a favorite of our staff. Make sure to double or triple the recipe! It's a great way to use up extra eggs when the chickens are laying heavily.

DUMPLINGS

1½ cups	flour	2 tsp	baking powder
¾ tsp	salt	1	egg, well beaten
2 T	oil or melted shortening		
1 cup	milk		

Mix dry ingredients in a medium bowl. Mix egg, oil, and milk in a small bowl. Pour into flour mixture and stir just until moistened. Drop by tablespoonfuls onto gently boiling stew. Cook uncovered 10 minutes. Cover and cook 10 minutes longer.

CRUST FOR MEAT PIES
This makes enough for a double crust pie.

2¼ cups	flour	¼ tsp	salt
2 T	butter	¼ cup	lard
1	egg yolk	3 T	cold water

Cream butter and lard. Cut in flour and salt. Add egg yolk and cold water.

MEAT PIE

2 cups	leftover meat or ground beef		
1	onion, chopped	2	carrots, diced
3	potatoes, cut in cubes	1 tsp	salt
double	pie crust *(above)*		

Place crust in the bottom of a pie plate. Fill with meat. Add top crust. Cut a vent opening to allow steam to escape. Place on a trivet in a Dutch oven. Bake until crust is browned. Serve warm.

FRUIT MINCEMEAT

1 cup	shredded suet
1 cup	light raisins
1 cup	dark raisins
3 med	green apples, peeled, cored, and chopped
½ cup	marmalade
¾ cup	chopped almonds
1 cup	brown sugar
1 cup	currants
5 oz	brandy
½	lemon, juiced
¼ tsp	grated nutmeg
½ tsp	ground ginger

Mix together the suet, raisins, apples, marmalade, almonds, sugar, and currants. Add the brandy, lemon juice, and spices. Cover the mixture with a cloth and leave it in the refrigerator overnight. Next day, mix throughly and use as pie filling. (Old storage method— place in a crock, cover with cloth and leave in the root cellar. Modern method—pack and seal in glass canning jars.) Many old recipes call for mixing with venison. The high sugar content helps to preserve the meat. Modern safety methods would require that this be canned in a pressure canner before storing.

Meat was often preserved by mixing with sugar and spices to form a mincemeat. Both raw and dried fruit were added to the meat. A crock of this could be stored several weeks in a root cellar. A common way to serve this preserved meat was as a mincemeat pie. The mincemeat purchased today is much sweeter and seldom contains meat. It has become a dessert, rather than a main course meat dish.

FISH

THE IMPORTANCE OF FISH and the reliance of all 18th-century residents of the Michilimackinac region upon the fisheries cannot be underestimated. Evidence of fishing is available through archaeology and from accounts of missionaries, explorers, French and British soldiers, fur traders, and voyageurs who passed through the area. Their records show that local populations relied heavily on the seasonal availability of sturgeon, whitefish, and lake trout. When writing journals or letters, everyone who passed through the straits area commented on fish and its importance as a food source.

Fish were much more reliable than crops. Farming depends on rich soil, good weather, and the number of frost-free days. The growing season at Mackinac is quite short for many plants. The last frost is usually in late May and the first frost in the fall often comes in early September. There are exceptions, such as the summer of 1993, when it actually snowed on the 4th of July! During the summer there are occasional storms, some with heavy winds, that can damage crops. During the summer of 1995 a windstorm knocked down much of the corn crop and 18 trees in the park.

The soil near the fort is very thin and sandy. The inhabitants of the fort did not come to build farms and homesteads. They came instead to gather furs, supply the voyageurs with trade goods, or garrison the fort. The difficulty and expense of transporting supplies for large numbers of soldiers and

traders made food valuable. If adequate amounts of fish could be caught locally, then they could supplement the food supplies that had to be brought in from Detroit or Montreal.

Fish were also important to the diet for religious purposes. From 1715-1760 Michilimackinac was occupied by French missionaries, traders, voyageurs, and their families. The French people were all Catholic and bound by church rules of fasting. "Meatless days" had been instituted by the church in prior centuries to encourage the practice of self-denial and also because there was a shortage of meat in Europe. Fasting made going without meat a respectful and pious act, rather than emphasizing the fact that meat was unaffordable or unavailable. Catholics had been trained from early childhood to avoid meat on Fridays, Saturdays, and the vigils of feast days.

Food was especially limited during the late winter Lenten season. Fall butchered animals had been used up, hunting was not productive in deep snow, the root cellars were emptying out, and the spring migrations of waterfowl had not yet started. The church called for 40 days of fasting and abstinence during this season — something that happened naturally because of food supplies. Altogether there were 140 meatless days in the Roman Catholic Church calendar during the eighteenth century. These included all Fridays, Saturdays, Lent and vigils of Holy Days. The fish caught at Mackinac would have been the main protein food available on these days of fasting.

BOILED WHITEFISH

Clean the fish (gut and scale). Cut into chunks or strips about two inches wide. Fish may also be cut into filets and skinned, if desired. Place in cold water; add seasonings such as salt, parsley, and onion, if desired. Bring to a boil and simmer on the side of the fireplace until the fish flakes easily. Serve warm.

PLANKED WHITEFISH

Season **whitefish** with **salt and pepper**. Heat an oak plank near the fire. **Oil** the fish and put it in the center of the board. Cover the exposed part of the plank with **coarse salt** to keep it from burning. Spread **bacon** on top of the fish, then prop the board in front of the fire and bake about 45 minutes.

BAKED STUFFED WHITEFISH[3]

2 ¹/₂ lbs	whitefish			salt and pepper
³/₄ cup	minced onion			flour
3 cups	fresh bread crumbs	1 tsp		thyme
¹/₄ tsp	salt	1		egg, slightly beaten
2 T	melted butter	¹/₂ cup		white wine
¹/₂ cup	water			

Clean and scale fish. Remove gills but leave fish whole. Make 3 or 4 gashes on the upper side of fish. Sprinkle with salt and pepper. Set aside.

Combine onion, bread crumbs, seasonings, egg, and butter, and mix well. Lightly stuff mixture into fish cavity and gashes. Sprinkle with flour. Bake until fish turns opaque and flakes easily. Remove fish from the pan and place on a platter.

A gravy can be made by adding water and wine to the pan. Heat and pour over fish.

Baron de LaHontan, upon visiting the Mackinac region, noted this about whitefish:

All sorts of Sauces spoil it, so that 'tis always eat either boil'd or broil'd, without any manner of seasonings. [2]

*A frightening story of one fishing trip is told about **Louis Hamelin**, who settled at Michilimackinac with his family after the end of the French-Indian War.*

"One winter day, while he was arranging the lines for trout fishing on Lake Michigan, a violent wind detached a piece of ice on which he was standing, and drove it far out into the Lake. He passed nine days in this perilous position, without nourishment and without shelter, exposed to the cold lake winds. Thanks to a favorable change, he was at length blown back to the shore upon this novel kind of a raft, after having many times despaired of his safety."[4]

COD

For many years fish, particularly cod, had been caught off the East Coast and shipped back to Europe. To preserve it for this sea voyage, the fish was salted and packed in barrels. In the earlier years at Michilimackinac, salt would not have been available in large enough quantities to do that kind of fish preservation locally. Some salt was brought in, but it was not until sailing ships brought salt by the barrel from Detroit that any quantity of fish would have been preserved by salting. By the 19th century, when the fort had been removed to Mackinac Island, salting barrels of fish was common practice. At the end of the fur trade era many Mackinac men found jobs in the fisheries that supplied Detroit and Chicago with numerous barrels of salted whitefish.

SALTED COD WITH GRAVY

1 lb	salt cod		boiling water to cover fish

GRAVY:

2 T	flour	2 oz	salt pork

Soak cod in cold water overnight. Next day, drain and place in a kettle and just cover with boiling water. Simmer, but do not boil. Cook until fish flakes easily, about 15 minutes. Save the cooking water.

To make gravy, cut salt pork into thin slices and fry until crisp. Add flour and blend well. Add 1 cup of the water in which fish was cooked and cook until thickened. Add fish and reheat. Serve warm.

FISH BALLS

3 lbs	fresh fish, boned	2 cups	water
4 cups	unpeeled, diced potatoes		
¼ tsp	pepper	2 T	oil
2 tsp	maple syrup	4 cups	oil for frying
	herbs to taste (dill, parsley, fennel)		

Boil fish and potatoes in a covered pot for 25 minutes. Drain and mash. Add remaining ingredients (except oil) and shape into 2-inch balls. Fry in hot oil, turning until golden brown. Drain and serve, hot or cold.

SALTED FISH CAKES

2 cups	freshened salt fish, boned		
6 med	potatoes	2	eggs, beaten
2 T	cream	2 tsp	chopped onion
	parsley		pepper
	melted butter		vegetable oil

Fish were often preserved by smoking them over a juniper or hickory fire. The smoke was contained in a smokehouse or barrel while the fish were drying.

To freshen salted fish: Place fish in water and soak overnight. Pour off water, reserving it for boiling potatoes.

   Boil potatoes in the water that the fish have soaked in. Mash them thoroughly and mix in the fish. Adjust the amount of potatoes to the amount of fish until a firm mixture is formed. Blend eggs into the potato-fish mixture. Stir in cream and add onion and parsley. Season with pepper to taste. Shape into small cakes and fry in melted butter and vegetable oil until golden brown.

Patrick Sinclair, 1780:

I have a Sergeant and six men employed in fishing & perhaps I may be able over & above Indian consumption, to send some thousand weight of fine trout to Niagara for the use of our brown allies there—we smoak it with juniper, after keeping it one night in salt. [5]

CULLEN SKINK [6]
Scottish Smoked Fish Soup

1½ lbs	smoked fish fillets	2 cups	milk
1 med	onion, chopped		
3½ cups	water	1 cup	diced raw potato
1 T	butter	1 cup	heavy cream
	salt and pepper	½ cup	fresh parsley

Put smoked fish in a large, shallow pan with milk, onion, and water. Bring slowly to a boil and remove from heat. Lift the fish out of the pan, skin and bone it, and flake it into small pieces. Set aside. Place the skin and bones in a saucepan with the cooking liquid and onion. Add potato and simmer for one hour.

Strain the stock through a sieve and return it to the saucepan. Heat thoroughly and add the fish, butter, and cream. Season to taste with salt and pepper and sprinkle parsley over the top just before serving.

FISH HASH

1 lb	fresh fish, boned and skinned
4 med	potatoes, boiled and cooled
¼ cup	butter or margarine
¾ cup	light cream
	salt and pepper to taste

Mince fish and set aside. Peel potatoes and dice in small cubes. Heat cream and butter in a soup kettle until butter melts, being careful not to scorch cream. Add the fish and cook 2 to 3 minutes, just until the fish turns opaque. Add potatoes and salt and pepper and continue cooking 3 to 5 minutes, just until thoroughly heated. Serve hot!

Finnian Haddie
A Scottish dish using salted or smoked fish in cream sauce

1 sm	onion, sliced in rings
2 lbs	smoked cod or haddock fillets
$1/4$ tsp	fresh black pepper
	water

Sauce:

2 T	unsalted butter	2 T	flour
2 cups	milk	$1/2$ cup	heavy cream
2 T	fresh lemon juice	1 tsp	Dijon mustard
1 tsp	dry mustard	3	egg yolks, beaten

Freshen fish by soaking in salt water for 1 hour.

Place onion rings in the bottom of a kettle. Place fish fillets on top and grind fresh black pepper over them. Cover them with water. Bring the water to a boil; then reduce heat and poach the fish, covered, for 10 to 15 minutes or until it flakes easily. Drain the fish, discard the onions, and separate the fillets into 1- to 2-inch pieces.

While fish is poaching, make the sauce. In a medium pan, over low heat, melt butter. Whisk in flour, and beat until the mixture has formed a smooth roux and is beginning to turn light brown. Slowly whisk in milk, beating well so that no lumps form. Cook sauce about 3 minutes, until it thickens. Stir in cream, lemon juice, and mustard. Remove sauce from heat, and cool slightly. Whisk in egg yolks, and blend well. Add flaked fish to sauce and mix well. Reheat over low heat. Serve warm over sippets of toast.

This may also be used as a sauce for crepes *(see page 81)*.

Peter Pond, 1773:

This Lake or Strate abounds in all sorts of fine fish. I have Wade a trout takeen in By Mr. Campo with a Hoock and lind under the Ice in March Sixtey Six Pounds wait. I was Present. The water was fifteen fatham Deape; the white fish are another Exqiuseat fine fish. Thay will way from 2 to 9 & 10 Pound wt. [8]

CAPILOTADE OF FISH[7]
Reheated Hashed Fish

1 lb	cod	2 T	butter
$1/4$ tsp	salt	$1/8$ tsp	ground cloves
$1/8$ tsp	nutmeg	$1/8$ tsp	ground ginger
2	scallions, chopped	$1/3$ cup	vinegar
$1/2$ cup	bread crumbs		butter

Fry fillets in butter for 10 minutes. Mix spices and scallions with bread crumbs. Layer fish with crumb mixture and dot with butter. Repeat. Sprinkle vinegar over the casserole. Cover and bake in a hot oven, 10-15 minutes. (To cook in the fire-place, place fish in a crock and steam crock in a Dutch oven.)

FISH PIRAGES
Fish Pie

Leftover fish or boiled whitefish

3	potatoes	1	onion
2	carrots		salt and pepper
	fresh or dried parsley		
	dry chicken bouillon for seasoning if desired		
double	pie crust *(see page 84)*		

Boil and debone fish. Cut up carrots, potatoes, onion, and parsley. Combine with the fish and set aside. Line a pie pan with dough. Place fish-potato mixture in pie pan, dot with butter, salt, and pepper. Cover with top crust and cut a slit to allow steam to escape. When baking in a Dutch oven, place a trivet on the bottom of the kettle. Preheat and place pie pan into hot oven. Place rimmed cover on top, set in hot ashes, and place more hot ashes on lid. Bake until done, about 40 minutes.

OPTIONAL: *Make individual fish pies by rolling dough into 9-inch circles, filling half full and folding edges over, like turnovers. Place in bottom of Dutch oven or on cookie sheet and bake till golden brown.*

TROUT FRIED IN OATMEAL
Traditional Scottish Breakfast

6	trout, cleaned		salt and pepper
2	eggs, beaten	1 cup	raw oatmeal
2 T	lard	2 T	butter

Wash trout; sprinkle the insides with salt.

Mix oatmeal with salt and pepper. Dip trout in beaten egg and then coat with oatmeal.

Melt lard in a pan and fry for 3 minutes on each side, until fish is crispy brown. Drain the grease and place the fish on a platter. Top with butter and serve.

DRIED FISH WITH SAUCE

5 lbs	dried fish	4	potatoes, peeled
5 strips	bacon	1	large onion, chopped
1 cup	heavy cream		white pepper

Simmer dried fish in water for 15 minutes. Remove fish to a platter, saving the water. Peel potatoes and boil them in the fish water until they are half cooked.

While potatoes are cooking, flake the fish and set to one side. Fry bacon and remove from the pan. Saute onions in the bacon fat until soft and transparent. Pour off excess fat.

When potatoes are half cooked, add flaked fish to the potatoes and water. Simmer. Crumble bacon into the pan of onions and add cream and white pepper. Warm cream but do not boil. Drain water, and place fish and potatoes on a platter. Pour the sauce over the top and serve warm.

Alexander Henry, 1762:

Trout are taken by making holes in the ice in which are set lines and baits. These are often left for many days together, and in some places at the depth of fifty fathoms; for the trout having swallowed the bait, remains fast and alive till taken up. This fish, which is found of the weight of from ten to sixty pounds and upward, constitutes the principal food of the inhabitants. When this fails they have recourse to maize, but this is very expensive. I bought more than a hundred bushels at forty livres per bushel. Money is rarely received or paid at Michilimackinac, the circulating medium consisting in furs and peltries. [9]

DRIED FISH WITH MAPLE SUGAR
This was a traditional Native American way to store dried fish.

When **fish** had been partly dried, the meat was removed from the bones. It was spread on a clean surface and worked by hand until it became a smooth, fine texture—like putty. **Maple sugar** was then worked into the mixture and it was stored in birchbark containers.

PICKLED FISH[10]

4-5 lbs	fish	1 T	chopped, fresh dill
3 cups	cider vinegar	12	peppercorns
2 med	onions, thinly sliced	1 T	wood ashes *(optional)*
12	dried juniper berries, crushed		

Whitefish and other fish can be pickled. Clean and cut into medium-sized pieces. Place in a crock on top of thin slices of onion. Simmer the cider vinegar with the juniper berries and seasonings. Stir in the wood ashes. Pour this mixture over the fish, adding more vinegar, if necessary, to cover. Cover the crock and let it stand in the refrigerator from 2 days to 2 weeks. After 2 days the vinegar and spices should have softened and dissolved all internal bones. Serve cold.

BAKED PICKLED HERRING

Clean and scale **fish**; do not bone. Cut into strips and place in a bean pot. Layer with **salt and pepper**. Add ¼ **cup of chopped raw salt pork** and **pickling spices** as desired. Cover with **cider vinegar**. Put lid on bean bot and bake slowly, 4-6 hours. The bones will dissolve with the slow baking and the vinegar.

Thousands of 18th-century artifacts, like this bone spear point, have been found by archaeologists at Michilimackinac. Every year since 1959 the archaeologists' trowels have peeled away the soil to reveal the buried past.

FISH JERKY

2-3 lbs	whitefish
1 tsp	pickling salt
1 tsp	allspice
1 T	pickling spice
2	bay leaves
2 med	onions, cut in rings
2T	distilled white vinegar

Combine salt, allspice, pickling spices, and bay leaves in a small bowl to make a dry cure.

Cut fish in strips ¼ inch thick. Soak the strips for 30 minutes in a cold brine, consisting of onions and vinegar, and **1 cup pickling salt** to **1 quart water**. Rinse fish strips in fresh water and place on a clean flat surface. Sprinkle both sides of each fish piece with the dry spices, using 1 T per 2 lbs fish. Place in a container and refrigerate 4-8 hours.

After the salt is absorbed, place the fish on drying racks or in a dehydrator. Dry 12-14 hours. Fish jerky should feel firm, dry, and tough, but not crumbly. For safety, store in refrigerator or freezer.

Lotbinière, 1749:

They catch their fish during the month of October at La Grosse Isle where they lay their nets, and after their winter supply of fish is caught they smoke it or put it in the snow to preserve it. [11]

BREADS

BREADS ARE MADE FROM GRAIN, a liquid, and some form of leavening. The flours of the time were usually wheat or ground cornmeal. Some of the wheat flour was imported from the Atlantic seaboard while some was grown at Detroit. Wheat farming was established at Detroit soon after Cadillac left Michilimackinac, and started a settlement there in 1701.

There is some mention of grain grown at Mackinac, during John Askin's time there. He planted both buckwheat and oats. It is quite possible that these were grown more for animal feed than for human consumption.

Flour was usually shipped in barrels on ships like the *Welcome* and *Felicity*. It came from Detroit and was stored in the King's Storehouse. Frequently contaminated with animal droppings and flour bugs, the flour was quite spoiled by spring. The purpose in sifting or "sieving" flour at this time was twofold: It separated the finer grain from the coarse grain, and separated the flour from meal worms.

It is likely the military bread was baked in one of the bake ovens located outside the land gate. It would take a lot of wood to heat up such an oven and would have been most efficient to bake a quantity at the same time. Individual families may also have used outdoor bake ovens, as these were common throughout Canada. Other breads were simply baked in the fireplace, either on a griddle or in a Dutch oven.

Outdoor bake ovens were built apart from houses and protected by a simple roof or cover. They were positioned so that prevailing winds would not blow smoke or sparks towards a house (or fort). They were often made of clay, but sometimes of brick or stone. A form of wood was constructed on a stone platform. This was covered with clay at least 8 inches thick. A door, possibly metal, was constructed at one end.

Dough was prepared in a wooden dough box with one or two divisions, on 4 legs. After the dough was kneaded, a lid would be tipped down to cover the box and shelter the dough while it rose. This top could also be used as a table. A week's worth of bread would be set to rise and meanwhile the oven would be fired up. Dry cedar, aspen, pine, and spruce made the hottest fire. Once the fire was reduced to embers, the coals were spread smooth and the oven closed up, until it was evenly heated. The embers were then raked out, the hearth swept clean and the loaves of risen dough were placed in it. The oven doors were closed up for about an hour and a half, until the bread made a hollow sound when struck on the bottom. After the completion of the bread baking, the ovens remained warm for 24 hours. This heat was useful for baking beans, desserts, and meat pies. The oven was also used to dry foods for winter. [2]

The 18th-century cook did not have the luxury of going to the store to purchase dried or cake yeast or baking powder. She needed to keep a starter going and use this to "set a sponge" the evening before baking. Such a starter could be made with leftover bread, hops, or potatoes. In a pinch she could add a little fireplace ash and some buttermilk, which acts like baking powder.

STARTERS

LIQUID HOP YEAST[3]

Liquid hop malt extract is available in stores that carry beer-making supplies. To make your own hop yeast try this recipe. Its taste resembles "beer bread."

1 cake	yeast	¼ cup	warm water
¼ tsp	sugar	3 med	potatoes
1 T	hop-flavored malt extract		
1 qt	boiling water	¼ cup	sugar

Dissolve yeast in lukewarm water; add ¼ tsp sugar. Set aside.

Add malt extract to boiling water. Scrub potatoes, but do not peel. Cut into small pieces and add to boiling water. Boil 10 minutes. Add ¼ cup sugar, mash, and drain off liquid.

Let cool until mixture is lukewarm. Add dissolved yeast cake. Let rise or work in a warm place for 6 hours. Pour into a jar and store in the refrigerator. Makes 1 quart (enough for 32 loaves). Keeps for months.

BREAD STARTER[4]

2 T	flour	1½ tsp	sugar
½ tsp	salt	2 cups	warmed milk

Combine ingredients; pour into a crock and leave in a warm place for 3-4 days, until it forms curds and smells slightly sour.

Save the bowl scrapings or a piece of dough to start the next batch and add milk or buttermilk as needed for liquid.

Askin diary, 1774:

April 27 Sowed Buck Wheat at the farm

April 28 also sowed Oates [at the farm]

May 7 Sowed Oates

May 10 Sowed the last Oats

May 28 Sowed Clover & Rye Grass

July 19 began to Cutt Hay

Aug 23 Reaped Some Oates

1775:

April 29 Sowed the large Garden at the Fort with Oats

May 1 Sowed the large Garden with Clover Seed to 66 foot Square

May 6 Sowed... Oats & Clover all this last Week at the farm

June 22 Sowed Buck Wheat

Buck Wheat may be Sowed the 20th of June on Land twice plowed where Pease have been the year before Oats may be sowd in old Turnip Ground. [1]

John Askin wrote to Detroit, 1778:

I hope you will at least be able to procure the greater part of the Corn & Flour I ordered & much of the former hulled, a Disa- pointment in these articles would in part knock up the North Trade & I assure you if less than three of four Vessells load of these things arrive this Season, some persons in that back country will perish & the trade be hurt, there is little or no dependance to be put on the grain that's to be got this way. [5]

STARTER BISCUITS

Add **1½ to 2 cups bread starter** to **4 cups flour** and **1 tsp baking soda**. Roll out on a floured board and cut into cir- cles with a glass or biscuit cutter. Bake 15 minutes in a Dutch oven. Makes 24 biscuits.

ASHCAKES
Hoe Cakes

1 cup	cornmeal	½ tsp	salt
	boiling water		

Mix cornmeal and salt in a small bowl. Gradually stir in boil- ing water to make a stiff dough. Mix thoroughly. Set aside to rest for several hours.

Form into small cakes about ½ inch thick and 4 inches in diameter. Place dough on a heavy hoe (garden hoe) prop- ped up by the fire and bake about 15 minutes, until firm.

OPTIONS: Brush the ashes from the hearth and place dough on a hot stone. You may cover them in corn husks or cabbage leaves if available. Cover with hot ashes, bake, and then brush off the ashes. Serve hot. Or bake on a griddle greased with lard. Turn with a spatula and bake until brown on both sides.

Corn

Cornbread

Combine:

1 cup	cornmeal	1 cup	flour
2 tsp	baking powder	½ tsp	salt
¼ cup	sugar (maple or white)		

Add:

1 cup	sourdough starter *(see page 117)*
1 cup	milk
1	egg
2 T	butter

Place the batter in the bottom of a Dutch oven. Bake about 20 minutes until the top is set and lightly browned.

If baking in a modern oven, place batter in a greased and floured cake pan or muffin tins and bake at 375°.

Cornmeal Pancakes

1 cup	cornmeal	2 T	sugar
1 tsp	salt	1 cup	boiling water
½ cup	flour	2 tsp	baking powder
1	egg	½ cup	milk
2 T	butter		

Combine cornmeal, sugar, and salt. Stir in water, cover and let set 10 minutes. Combine flour and baking powder; set aside. Beat liquids, add dry ingredients, and stir quickly.

Cook on a griddle. Serve with honey, maple syrup, or applesauce.

CORN PONE

¼ cup lard is a lump the size of an egg.

2 cups	cornmeal	1 tsp	salt
¼ cup	lard	2 cups	boiling water

Mix cornmeal and salt in a bowl. Cut in lard until mixture is crumbly. Add boiling water to moisten corn. Pat the dough into circles and bake in a Dutch oven or on a griddle, or wrap it in corn husks and bake it in the ashes.

HASTY PUDDING

This cornmeal mush was a favorite.

1 cup	cold water	½ cup	cornmeal
½ tsp	salt	2 cups	boiling water

Mix cornmeal with cold water. Add with salt to boiling water. Cook slowly, 10-15 minutes, stirring often. Serve with cream, maple sugar, honey, or molasses.

Chill and slice any unused mush, dust with flour, and fry in bacon grease. Serve with syrup.

HOMINY CAKES

1 cup	cooked hominy cereal		
1 egg,	beaten	1 T	butter
½ tsp	salt		
1 cup	uncooked hominy cereal		

Combine first four ingredients and stir until well mixed. Stir uncooked hominy into the batter. Pat dough out evenly on the bottom of a greased Dutch oven. Bake 30-40 minutes, until brown. Serve warm with butter.

BROWN BREAD

Serve with baked beans.

1 cup	rye flour	1 cup	cornmeal (Indian meal)
½ cup	wheat flour	1 cup	milk
½ cup	molasses	1 tsp	salt
1 tsp	baking soda	1 T	lard

Measure dry ingredients into a bowl. In a second bowl, mix milk, lard, and molasses. Add to dry ingredients and stir for 3 minutes. Place in a greased bowl and steam for 3 hours. To steam, place bowl on a trivet in a Dutch oven. Place an inch or two of water in oven. Cover and bake slowly.

A barrel of flour weighed 196 lbs. When made into bread it would produce about 265 lbs. of bread.[6]

BROWN BREAD WITH MAPLE SYRUP

2 cups	cornmeal	1 cup	rye flour
1 cup	white flour	1 cup	sour milk
1½ tsp	baking soda	1 cup	maple syrup
1 cup	fresh milk	½ cup	raisins

Dissolve soda in sour milk (1 cup milk and 1 T vinegar). Mix dry ingredients and add all the milk. Add maple syrup and raisins. Pour into a greased crock or mold and steam 2 hours. Serve hot with baked beans!

A modern cook can use a copper mold or even a coffee can to steam bread. Grease and flour the mold. Fill the mold ⅔ full of batter. Cover the top with parchment paper or aluminum foil that is tied on with twine.

Set the mold in a large pan or kettle with a lid. Pour boiling water ½ way up the mold. Cover kettle and steam on top of the stove. Add more water as it boils away.

OATS

BANNOCKS OR OATCAKES
Scottish quickbread, dating back to the 14th century

²/₃ cup   **medium oatmeal** *(try the oatmeal flours now available in health food supplies)*
2 tsp   **melted fat, oil, or bacon drippings**
pinch   **salt**
pinch   **baking soda** *(woodash is traditional)*
¹/₄ cup   **hot water**

Mix oatmeal, salt, and soda in bowl. Make a well in the middle and pour in fat. Stir and add enough water to make a stiff paste.

Spread some oatmeal on a board and knead the dough on it, using more oatmeal as necessary.

Roll out to ¹/₄ inch thickness and shape in a circle, using a dinner plate. Sprinkle dry oatmeal on the surface. Cut in quarters (farls) and place on a warm, greased griddle. Cook until the edges curl.

Michilimackinac was the hub of British activity in the upper Great Lakes during the American Revolution. Sixteen-foot high wooden stockades surrounded the village. Eighty British soldiers defended the post. The soldiers were housed in the barracks but the officers occupied houses alongside their fur trading neighbors. The bell of Ste. Anne's church summoned the French Catholic residents to worship or to wedding celebrations.

Only a few hundred people remained at Michilimackinac during the bleak winter. When summer came the Indians and traders returned for a lively season of trade and merriment. Camped on the beach,ß they traded furs and stories. Many had paddled their birch bark canoes for a month or more to reach Mackinac.

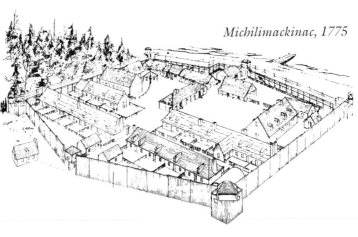

Michilimackinac, 1775

Bere Bannocks
Barley muffins from the Orkney Islands

Askin diary, 1774:

Tuesday Aug 23d
Reaped Some Oates[7]

1 cup	warm water		
1 tsp	light molasses or maple syrup		
1 cup	barley flour	¼ cup	flour
½ tsp	salt	1½ tsp	baking powder

Sift dry ingredients into a large bowl. Mix ½ cup of the water with the molasses or syrup. Stir into flour mixture. Add remaining water slowly, making a soft dough.

Place on a floured board and form into 6 balls. Flatten each ball to one-inch thickness.

Heat a griddle and sprinkle it with flour. Cook bannocks until browned, about 10 minutes. Flip and cook the other side.

Serve warm with butter, jam, or honey.

Oatmeal Bread

3 cups	flour	1¼ cups	oats
1½ tsp	baking powder	1 T	salt
1	egg	¼ cup	honey
1½ cups	milk	1 T	butter

Mix dry ingredients. In another bowl, beat egg, honey, and milk. Pour into oat mixture and stir just until moistened. The batter will be lumpy. Pour into a pan and bake 1 hour and 15 minutes.

POTATO

BOXTY
Scottish Potato Pancake

2 lbs	potatoes	4 cups	flour
	salt and pepper	¼ cup	melted butter

Boil and mash half the potatoes. Grate the other half coarsely; drain. Mix potatoes together.

Add flour, salt, and pepper, mixing well. Add melted butter; knead lightly. Make into 4 rounds 1 inch thick. Score into quarters.

Bake in a Dutch oven for 45-60 minutes until brown on top and cooked inside.

POTATO BREAD

½ cup	lukewarm water (90-115°)		
1 tsp	sugar	1 package	dry yeast
1 cup	mashed potatoes	1 cup	warm water
2 tsp	salt	3 T	sugar
3 T	oil	5-6 cups	flour

Add 1 tsp sugar to ½ cup water. Stir in yeast and set aside to work. Beat 1 cup warm water into mashed potatoes, until smooth. Add sugar, salt and oil. Beat in flour gradually. Add yeast, turn out onto a floured board and knead until smooth and elastic. Place in a Dutch oven in a warm place, and let rise until doubled in bulk. Cover and put oven in the coals. Replace coals on lid as necessary. Bake about 45 minutes, until browned and the loaf sounds hollow when tapped.

PRATIE SCONES
Potato Pancakes

1 cup	warm mashed potatoes (instant potatoes will work)		
⅓ cup	melted butter	1 tsp	salt
½ cup	flour		

Mix ingredients well. Divide the dough into thirds. Roll out each third (¼ inch thick) into a circle on a floured board. Score into pie-shaped wedges.

Bake on a griddle until both sides are lightly browned. Serve hot with syrup and melted butter, or cold with jam.

WHEAT

FRENCH BREAD

In a small bowl mix :

1 pkg	yeast	2 T	sugar
1¾ cups	lukewarm water		

In a big bowl mix:

6 cups	flour	1 tsp	salt

Add liquid and stir until an elastic dough is formed. Rub with butter and let rise. Punch, shape, place in a kettle, and let rise again. Bake 45 minutes or less. For a hard crust, brush the top with 1 T cornstarch, 1 T sugar, 2 T cold water.

This will make a round loaf because the kettle is round. If making in a modern oven use two 8" x 4½" bread pans.

John Askin to Philip Dejean at Detroit, June 4, 1778:

I was favoured with yours of the 24th of May last, the Mualtoe woman shall be disposed off agreeable to your desire so soon as Monsr Cerre or Monsr Degrosolier arrives; my famely is too numerous to keep her in my own house, & at present we want Bread more than Cooks. I have put her at Mr Mumforton's at present.

Mrs Askin presents her Compliments. [11]

A crude form of baking powder or baking soda was made by using a small amount of fireplace ash. When buttermilk was added, gas was released which caused the biscuit to rise. Cream of tartar was also available in the 1770s. Baking powder is a mixture of baking soda and cream of tartar.

BAKING POWDER BISCUITS

2 cups	flour	3 tsp	baking powder
1 tsp	salt	$1/3$ cup	shortening
$3/4$ cup	milk		

Mix dry ingredients. Cut shortening into mixture. Add milk and stir quickly. Turn out on a floured board. Roll out the dough to $3/4$ inch thick and cut with a biscuit cutter. Bake at 450° for 12-15 minutes.

DROP BISCUITS—Increase milk to 1 cup. Do not knead. Drop by tablespoonfuls and bake 10 minutes.

BEATEN BISCUITS—Leave out baking powder. Work dough 20 minutes on a floured board by beating with a rolling pin, folding and refolding until dough is blistered and pops.

IRISH SODA BREAD

1 cup	unbleached flour
4 cups	whole wheat flour
$1/2$ cup	rolled oats (not instant)
1 tsp	baking soda
1 tsp	salt
$2^1/2$ cups	buttermilk

Mix together flour, oats, soda, and salt. Gradually beat in 2 cups buttermilk to form a soft dough. Add more if needed.

Turn onto a floured board and knead lightly. Shape into a loaf, score the top into quarters, and bake in a Dutch oven at 375° for 40-50 minutes until golden brown.

MUFFINS

2 cups	flour	1/4 cup	sugar
3 tsp	baking powder	1/2 tsp	salt
1 cup	milk	1/3 cup	salad oil
1	egg, slightly beaten		

Mix dry ingredients in a large bowl. Mix liquid ingredients in a second bowl. Pour liquid into dry ingredients and mix quickly until moist. Do not beat. The batter will be lumpy. Bake at 400° for 20-25 minutes. Instead of muffin pans we pour the batter into a cake tin or right into the Dutch oven. It bakes in one piece and is sliced like a pie.

BAPS
Scottish Yeast Rolls

4 cups	flour, sifted	1 tsp	salt
2 T	lard	1 package	dry yeast
1 tsp	sugar	1 cup	warm milk

Mix flour and salt in a bowl. Mix sugar and yeast together in another bowl. Melt lard and add half the milk. Make a well in the middle of the flour and add yeast, lard, and remaining milk, mixing well with a wooden spoon or hands. Knead until smooth. Cover and let rise one hour.

Turn onto a floured board, knead lightly a second time, and form oval shapes about 3 inches long and 2 inches wide. Brush with milk and dust with flour. Let rise in a Dutch oven, about 15 minutes. Make a small dent in the top and then place in the fireplace over very hot coals (400°).

Bake 15 minutes or until done.

John Askin to McGill, Frobisher, and Patterson at Montreal, 1778:

I shall send a Vessell to Millwakee in search of Corn. I have 150 Bushells already there & hope for more. I have about 200 here & I shall send a Batteaux to Detroit that will bring me at least 120 Bushells. [8]

Welcome *Logbook*:

Saturday 5th Febr 1780 People employed as yester-day, except Finnigan who was this day Baking for the Party. [9]

BROWN BREAD

If you would like to make a bread with the bran that is removed in modern milling, use a blend of whole wheat and un-bleached white and add bran. (The bran is sold in the hot cereal area of modern grocery stores.)

1 cup	bran	$^3/_4$ cup	lukewarm water
4$^1/_2$ cups	white, unbleached flour		
3 cups	whole wheat flour	$^1/_4$ cup	molasses
1$^1/_2$ cups	lukewarm water	2 T	melted shortening
1 T	salt	1 T	dry yeast
$^1/_4$ cup	warm water		

Soak bran in $^3/_4$ cup warm water. Sift flours together. Add bran, mixing well.

Dissolve molasses in 1$^1/_2$ cups lukewarm water and add melted shortening and salt.

Dissolve yeast in $^1/_4$ cup warm water and stir into the liquid mixture. Add liquid to the flour mixture. Knead thoroughly. Let rise overnight in a warm place in a large bowl. Punch down and shape into a loaf. Let rise again in a large Dutch oven until double in bulk. Bake 1 hour, or until the loaf sounds hollow when tapped.

RAISIN BREAD

1 pkg	yeast	2$^1/_2$ cups	warm water
2 tsp	salt	2 tsp	cinnamon
$^1/_2$ cup	honey	2 cups	raisins
6-7 cups	flour		

Mix 3 cups of the flour with salt and cinnamon. Dissolve yeast in 1 cup of the warm water and pour into flour mixture. Add honey and raisins. Add remaining flour and water. Knead 10 minutes. Let rise. Bake at 350° for 1 hour.

NUTBREAD

2½ cups	flour	3 tsp	baking powder
½ tsp	salt	1	egg, beaten
1 tsp	vanilla	¾ cup	sugar
¼ cup	butter	1¼ cups	milk
1 cup	chopped walnuts		

Mix flour, baking powder, and salt. Set aside. Beat egg. Add vanilla. Cream butter and sugar. Add egg mixture. Add milk. Stir in dry ingredients. Fold in walnuts. Pour into a greased cast iron kettle or a large greased and floured bread pan.

Bake at 375° for 60-65 minutes. Cool in the pan. Remove to a rack to cool completely before slicing.

VARIATION: Add dried fruit, raisins, etc.

SALLYLUNN

Sweetbread, used like a coffee cake

2 cups	flour	2 tsp	baking powder
½ tsp	salt	2	eggs, separated
½ cup	sugar	¾ cup	milk
3 T	melted butter		

Sift flour, baking powder, and salt. Beat egg yolks and beat in sugar. Add dry ingredients and milk; stir in melted butter. Beat egg whites until stiff and fold into batter. Pour into a 9" cake pan and place on a trivet in a Dutch oven. Cover with the lid and bake in the ashes until golden brown. Cool on a rack or serve warm.

John Askin to Sampson Fleming at Detroit, April 28, 1778:

I will follow Your advice & not have any Provisions Actually Condemned, un-till I see when we can get others, however what is not fit for Serving I shall lay one side, our flour is realy very bad, if what you sent had reached us it would have done much Service by mixing it with the other flour. [10]

Several versions call for lemon peel, raisins, currants, almonds, and spices. Many recipes call for it to be baked in a tube pan (angelfood cake pan) but we have no reference to those being used at Mackinac.

Apple Cinnamon Bread
This is like a coffee cake.

Dough:

2 cups	sifted flour	2 tsp	baking powder
½ tsp	salt	½ tsp	sugar
2 T	butter	1	egg, beaten
1 cup	milk		

Topping:

1 cup	brown sugar	4 T	softened butter
½ tsp	cinnamon		apples, peeled and sliced

Mix flour, baking powder, and salt. Cream sugar with butter. Add beaten egg and milk. Stir in flour mixture. Pour the batter into a greased cast iron kettle or a 9" round cake pan. Mix brown sugar, butter, and cinnamon in a bowl. Sprinkle on batter and place apples on top. Bake at 425° for 35 minutes.

Pumpkin or Squash Bread

4	eggs	2 cups	sugar
1 cup	oil	3½ cups	flour
1 tsp	salt	1½ tsp	baking soda
1 tsp	cinnamon	¾ tsp	baking powder
1 cup	chopped walnuts	1 cup	raisins
3 tsp	vanilla		
2 cups	canned, frozen or grated pumpkin or squash		

Beat eggs well. Add sugar and oil. In a second bowl, combine flour, salt, baking soda, cinnamon, and baking powder. Mix dry ingredients with liquid. Add squash. Add walnuts, raisins, and vanilla. Pour into a greased 10" Dutch oven and bake at 375° about 1 hour, until firm.

SCONES

2-3 cups	unbleached flour	1 tsp	baking soda
2 tsp	cream of tartar	¼ tsp	salt
4 T	butter	¾ cup	milk

Sift flour, soda, cream of tartar, and salt. Cut in butter until mixture is crumbly. Form a well in the center and pour in milk. Mix until a soft dough forms. Be careful not to over-mix.

Knead dough lightly on a floured board. Pat into a circle about ¾ inch thick. Cut into circles with a glass or biscuit cutter. Bake scones in a preheated Dutch oven about 10 minutes, until they rise and are golden brown.

VARIATIONS:

Cheese Scones: Add 1 cup grated cheese.

Chive Scones: Add a handful of fresh, chopped chives.

Herb Scones: Add 2 tsp fresh or 1 tsp dried herbs (tarragon, parsley, oregano, seasoned salt).

Jam Scones: Make basic dough. Roll into 2 circles. Spread the bottom circle with 2 T jam. Brush the edges with milk. Place the second circle of dough on top and seal. Brush the top with beaten egg and bake in a Dutch oven.

Onion Scones: Chop a small mild onion and cook until transparent. Add to dough before rolling out. Brush the tops of the scones with beaten egg and garnish with bits of onion before baking.

Raisin Scones: Add 1 cup raisins and sprinkle the tops of the scones with cinnamon and sugar before baking.

Treacle Scones: Add 2 T molasses to milk before adding to flour. Add 1 cup chopped walnuts.

A sweeter tea scone

3 cups flour
4 tsp baking powder
1 tsp salt
½ cup sugar
⅔ cup shortening
⅔ cup raisins
1 egg, beaten
1¼ cups sour milk
½ tsp soda

SINGING HINNIES
Scones

1½ cups flour		½ tsp	salt
1 tsp	baking powder	4 T	butter
4 T	lard	⅔ cup	buttermilk
⅓ cup	heavy cream (whipping cream)		
3 T	currants or raisins		

Sift flour, salt, and baking powder. Cut lard and butter into flour mixture. Add buttermilk and cream to make a soft dough. Add currants.

Roll out the dough (¼ inch thick) on a floured board or cloth. Cut into circles with a glass, cup, or biscuit cutter. Bake on a hot griddle until browned. Turn and cook the other side. Makes 1 dozen.

The name of this dish comes from the sound of butter and cream sizzling on the griddle.

SHORT'NING BREAD

½ cup	butter	¼ cup	light brown sugar
1½ cups	flour		

Cream butter and sugar. Add flour and mix well. Roll out ½ inch thick on a floured board. Use a glass to cut into circles. Bake in a Dutch oven 15-20 minutes. Sprinkle with sugar before serving. Some recipes call for the batter to be moistened with an egg yolk and milk.

Traditionally eaten at Christmas time. A Scottish custom was to offer this bread to the first guest to enter your house on New Year's day.

SOURDOUGH BREAD

2 cups	starter *(see page 117)*		
1 pkg	yeast *(optional, for insurance and speed)*		

Add:

4 cups	flour	2 T	sugar
1 tsp	salt	2 T	melted fat

Place dry ingredients in a bowl. Add 1T of the fat and mix well. Add remaining fat to starter and mix well. Pour into flour. Knead for 10 minutes. Place in a Dutch oven and let rise about 2 hours. Bake for 50-60 minutes.

SOURDOUGH HOTCAKES

2 cups	starter *(see page 117)*		
1 or 2	eggs	1 tsp	baking soda
1 tsp	salt	1 T	sugar
2T	oil		

Blend starter, eggs, soda, salt, and sugar together. Add oil.

Grease a griddle. Drop by ¼ cup onto hot griddle. When bubbles rise to the surface, turn, and bake the other side. Serve with butter and maple syrup.

Sourdough Starter

1 pkg	dry yeast	1 cup	warm water
2 tsp	salt	4 T	sugar
1¹/₂ cups	white flour		

Soak yeast in warm water. Add salt, sugar and flour. Stir well and store in a covered bowl, in a warm place. (The top of a water heater is great!)

When planning to bake next day, add 1 cup lukewarm water and 1 cup flour. Leave at room temperature overnight.

If not using, refrigerate. Take out the day before needed; let come to room temperature. Add 1 cup each flour and water.

SOURDOUGH MUFFINS

2 cups starter *(see page 117)*

1½ cups	flour	½ cup	sugar
1 tsp	salt	¼ cup	dry milk
1 tsp	baking soda	1 cup	raisins *(optional)*
½ cup	melted fat	1 or 2	eggs

Mix dry ingredients in a large bowl. Mix liquid ingredients in a second bowl. Pour liquid into dry ingredients. Mix quickly until moist. Do not beat; the batter will be lumpy. Bake at 375° for 30-35 minutes.

We bake them in a Dutch oven. Just pour the batter in and bake like a cake. Cut into pie-shaped wedges and serve. At home you can bake them in muffin tins.

Wafers

French Catholic clergy made Communion wafers in a wafer iron. Mackinac State Historic Parks has the original Ste. Anne wafer iron in our collection. These irons have two flat molds with long handles, hinged together like a giant pair of scissors. The iron was heated up in the fireplace. The batter (simply flour and water) was poured into the mold, and the iron closed. The heat would cook the wafers. These were tipped out, the iron reheated and the process repeated until sufficient were prepared.

Vegetables and Fruits

THE MOST IMPORTANT CROP used at Mackinac was corn. This grain was the mainstay of the voyageur's diet as he paddled off to winter in the West. It was a food that traveled well and could be prepared in many ways. It was pounded into meal, baked into bread, and most often served as a porridge called sagamity. It could be stored for months and was easily transported by canoe. This corn was grown primarily by the Ottawa and was traded to the French and British.

The diary made by John Askin in 1774-75 tells us about crops and vegetables at Michilimackinac. Askin had been granted land near today's French Farm Lake, where he planted vegetables, especially potatoes, and kept some animals. He also planted large gardens outside the fort. Askin employed some French-Canadian men and had several slaves who did much of the physical work, although he writes as if he also worked in the garden daily. The soldiers maintained gardens, too, for the use of the British military.

At Colonial Michilimackinac we have nine gardens, including a soldier's garden, an herbal garden, and several gardens behind individual households. We also have animal pens where visitors can see sheep, cows, a horse, chickens, ducks, and geese. We use heritage varieties of seeds whenever they are available. It is sometimes difficult to identify and find sources of appropriate 18th-century varieties, particularly as there is no listing of varieties used at Mackinac. The seed references for this site are general, simply listing items such as beans, cabbage, and corn. The only record of seed purchase is this letter from James Sterling to James Syme, from the James Sterling Letterbook, dated Detroit, 15 July 1762. It states, "Mr Porteous arrived here Last Night

Askin inventory, 1776:
He lists the tools that
he had for use. These
were mostly hand tools,
except for the plows and
the "Machine for
cutting Oats".

a new sett of Plow Irons

an Old Plow with Irons

A Corn Mill partly Used

A New London Corn Mill
  not yet Arrived

1 very large weighing
  Beam

1 small Ditto

A Machine for cutting
  Oats

2 Common Scythes

a Garden Hoe

6 Spades and Shovels

a Hay fork

a Watering Pott

An Iron Garden Rake

a Turkey whetstone

2 Hulling Basketts

30 lb of Peril Barley

a Keg of Clover Seed

1½ Bushell of Barley

1 bag of Beans

1 Bushell of Oats

5 Barrells of Lime

3 Barrells of Vinegar
  making [1]

from Niagara & brought with him two Kegs of Powder a Box of Garden Seeds & thirty one of the french Blankets." [2]

Fortunately, many people have developed an interest in historic agriculture and are actively promoting the saving of old varieties of seeds. Several museums and organizations have these available through special seed-saving programs. We use those that seem appropriate to the 18th century and this climate, and have an historical reference. If seeds can be identified as being in use in Montréal and Québec, or through the Albany/Niagara/Detroit trade routes, we assume they were available at Mackinac. The climates are similar and the fort supplies all came through these places. There are several seed sources listed at the end of this book, which the historic gardener can use. These are especially fun for those involved in reenactments or who work at historic sites.

The active archaeology program conducted each summer at Michilimackinac has helped us to find and identify many seeds. One study written by Richard Ford analyzes the corn found by archaeologists at Mackinac. A collection of 35 broken corn cobs, excavated under the direction of Dr. Lyle Stone, were determined to be of the Eastern Complex maize. Two of the cobs had rows of 10 kernels and the rest were eight-kernel rows. They were smaller than those found in southern Michigan which was probably due to the weather and the shorter growing season. [3]

Other field crops used by fort residents were beans, peas, potatoes, cabbage, onions, lettuce, radishes, pumpkins, squash, and melons. They also made use of wild fruits and berries that grew in the area. The Chippewa harvested wild rice, although that was more common further north, in the Lake Superior Region. The one domestic fruit was the apple, which was grown by the Askins. Wheat was imported from Detroit or other Eastern settlements. Some of these foods were grown by fort residents and others by the Ottawa at L'Arbre Croche (Cross Village, Michigan).

CORN

Alexander Henry wrote this about the Indian corn:

"L'Arbre Croche is the seat of the Jesuit mission of St. Ignace de Michilimackinac...The missionary resides on a farm attached to the mission and situated between the village and the fort, both of which are under his care. The Ottawa of L'Arbre Croche. . . grow maize for the market of Michili-mackinac , where this commodity is depended upon for provisioning the canoes. [4]

"The village of L'Arbre Croche supplies, as I have said, the maize, or Indian corn, with which the canoes are victualed. This species of grain is prepared for use by boiling it in a strong lye, after which the husk may be easily removed; and it is next mashed and dried.   In this state it is soft and friable like rice. The allowance for each man on the voyage is a quart a day; and a bushel with two pounds of prepared fat is reckoned to be a month's subsistence. No other allowance is made of any kind, not even of salt; and bread is never thought of. The men, nevertheless, are healthy and capable of performing their heavy labor. This mode of victualing is essential to the trade, which being pursued at great distances, and in vessels so small as canoes, will not admit of the use of other food. If the men were to be supplied with bread and pork the canoes could not carry a sufficiency for six months; and the ordinary duration of the voyage is not less than fourteen. The difficulty which would belong to an attempt to reconcile any other men than Canadians to this fare seems to secure to them and their employers the monopoly of the fur trade." [5]

CORN PUDDING

1 dozen	ears fresh sweet corn (4 cups grated corn)
	cream or evaporated milk
4	eggs, lightly beaten

1$\frac{1}{2}$ tsp	salt	$\frac{1}{2}$ tsp	pepper
2 T	sugar	6 T	melted butter

Husk corn and remove the silk. Place in a colander over a bowl. Use a sharp knife and slice off the tops of the kernels, scraping the pulp into the bowl. Leave the scraped corn in the colander so the milk from the corn can drip into the bowl. Measure the liquid and add enough cream to make 1 cup. Combine with remaining ingredients and fold in corn. Pour into a crock. Place crock on a trivet in a Dutch oven and cover. Set on coals, cover lid with coals, and bake 1 hour or until set. (You can substitute canned creamed corn.)

CORN CUSTARD

2 cups	corn, fresh or canned		
1 tsp	sugar	1 tsp	salt
$\frac{1}{4}$ cup	flour	3	eggs, beaten well
2 cups	milk	2 T	melted butter
	pepper to taste		

Mix corn with dry ingredients. Add milk, eggs, and butter. Bake in a crock set on a trivet in a Dutch oven. Pour water in the bottom of the oven so the custard will steam. Bake about 60 minutes, until a knife inserted comes out clean.

CORN FRITTERS

2 cups	fresh green corn		
2	eggs, separated	$^1/_4$ cup	cream
$^1/_4$ cup	flour	$^1/_2$ tsp	salt
$^1/_2$ tsp	pepper	$^1/_2$ cup	lard

Grate fresh corn into a bowl. Beat egg yolks slightly. Add cream, flour, salt, and pepper. Stir in corn. Beat egg whites until stiff. Gently fold into corn mixture. Melt lard in a shallow Dutch oven or fry pan. Drop in tablespoonfuls of fritter batter and fry. Turn until both sides are golden brown. Drain and serve hot. (You can substitute canned creamed corn.)

WHITPOT OR SWEETENED CORNMEAL PUDDING

$2^1/_2$ T	cornmeal	2 T	cold milk
2 cups	scalded milk	$^1/_2$ cup	sugar
$^1/_2$ tsp	salt	1	egg, beaten
$^1/_4$ cup	cold milk	1 T	butter

Wet cornmeal with 2 T cold milk; let stand. Meanwhile, scald 2 cups milk, and add cornmeal, sugar, and salt. Place ingredients in a crock and set crock in a kettle of hot water. This forms a double boiler and prevents the milk from scorching. Cook, covered over hot water, for 20-30 minutes. Mix beaten egg with $^1/_4$ cup cold milk. Slowly pour into cornmeal mixture, stirring. Remove from heat and serve. Garnish bowl with butter.

Askin inventory, 1776-78:

Stages for drying Corn

2 large Kittles in a furnace at Waterside

a Corn Mill partly Used

A New London Corn Mill not yet Arrived

a Turkey whetstone

2 Hulling Basketts [6]

Some Europeans called corn "turkey wheat." When it was introduced into Europe it was considered an exotic food. Most exotic items came from the Far East through Turkey. During the 18th century most Europeans did not recognize it as a North American food.

HULLED CORN

Hulled corn was made from flint or Indian corn. Lye was made using wood ash and water. To make a batch, first boil a **shovelful of sifted hardwood ash** with a kettle of water. We always use the same kettle because the lye pits it. The kettle should not be used for other food. The lye is strong enough when it will float an egg. Add a **quart of dry corn** to the lye solution and boil until the hulls loosen (about an hour). Pour through a colander and rinse thoroughly. Place colander in a large bowl of **water** and let it soak. Rub the kernels between your hands to loosen hulls. Repeat rinses until hulls are removed and the hominy is left. It can be used as fresh hominy at this stage. Most of the corn at Mackinac was dried on drying stages or racks and packed in bags for the voyageurs to take out on their fur trade trips.

Jonathan Carver wrote in 1766:

They conducted us to their village, gave us plenty of green corn, beans & squash, and fish with a sort of bread made of the corn in the milk squeezed and pounded together and baked under the ashes.[7]

SUCCOTASH

The Indian name for this dish was "misickquatash." They combined whatever meat was available with corn and whatever kinds of beans were grown in the area. In the 19th century many recipes also called for tomatoes, but in the 18th century most folks thought tomatoes were poisonous and only used them as ornamental plants.

2 cups	cooked lima beans	2 cups	cooked corn
2 T	butter		salt

Cook beans and corn separately ahead of time. Mix ingredients together and warm in a kettle. Do not overcook. The beans and corn should still retain their shape. Many versions call for salt pork to be added.

CORN COOKED IN HUSKS

Soak **corn**, with the husks on, in a bucket of water for 2 hours. Bury corn in coals of fire and bake till tender. Peel back husks, remove cornsilk, and add butter and salt. Eat from the cob.

BEANS

Domestic peas and common beans (*Phaseolus vulgaris*) have been identified by archaeologists at Michilimackinac.[9] These could have been haricot beans such as Great Northern, small whites, navy, white kidney, flageolets (immature kidney beans), pink beans, kidney beans, or cranberry beans. Many of these were also known under different regional names. Peter Kalm dates scarlet runner beans to 1750 in the American colonies. This variety was imported from India by British officers serving abroad. Jacob's cattle or trout bean dates to the 18th century and was very common in New England. These were usually grown for the dry shelled beans for soup. The Kentucky wonder pole bean also traces its lineage to the 18th century. We use a variety of these beans at Mackinac.

   We plant the beans in two ways. The bush beans are planted in rows in raised garden beds. They are staked with "peabrush" or tied up with strings. The pole beans are supported by fences, poles, or, most often, by cornstalks. This was the Indian way. It has a dual purpose, because the beans add nitrogen to the soil, which the corn needs, and the cornstalks support the beans so the pods don't rot on the ground. The bean vines also help support the corn when a west wind blows in off Lake Michigan!

Askin diary, 1774:

May 28th Sowed Garden Pease, Beans, Clover & Rye Grass [8]

BAKED BEANS

During the 18th century many folks had outdoor bake ovens. After a day's baking, the oven would still be warm. It was common to put in a pot of beans after the breads and pies had baked. The oven would stay warm for several hours and was perfect for baking beans.

Another option is to bury the pot in a hole and let it simmer all day. To do this, bring the beans and water to a boil over an open fire. In the meantime prepare a hole in the ground twice as big as the bean pot. Build a fire and when it is reduced to coals, add the bean pot. Add salt pork, sweetening, and spices to the beans. Cover tightly. Bury the pot in the hole and let them simmer all day.

1 lb	beans	1 cup	brown sugar
1 tsp	dry mustard		salt
1/4 tsp	pepper	1/4 lb	salt pork
1 med	onion		
1/4 cup	dark molasses or maple syrup		

Soak beans overnight; drain. Add the other ingredients. Cover with water. Bake in a covered Dutch oven for several hours, until beans are tender. If beans go dry, add more water. (A ceramic covered bean pot may also be used and set in the ashes on the side.)

If you forget to soak the beans ahead, a hurry-up tip is to boil them in soda water until the skins start to split, drain, and then follow directions for baked beans. This does tend to make the beans rather mushy and darkens their color.

MAPLE BAKED BEANS

6 cups	water	2 cups	dry beans
1 stick	cinnamon	1 1/2 tsp	salt
1/3 cup	maple sugar	1/4 cup	vinegar
4 T	maple syrup		

Cover beans with water and bring to a boil for 4 minutes. Remove from heat, cover, and let sit 1 hour. Add cinnamon and salt. Cover and simmer 2 hours, until beans are tender. Add more water if it starts to go dry. Stir in maple sugar and vinegar. Bake 30 minutes more. Top with maple syrup and serve.

Boston Baked Beans

1 quart	soaked red kidney beans		
1 cup	maple syrup	$^1/_4$ lb	salt pork
$^1/_4$ cup	chili sauce	1 sm	onion
$^1/_8$ tsp	pepper	$^1/_4$ tsp	dry mustard
1 tsp	ginger		salt

Score salt pork and add to beans. Mix $^1/_2$ cup of the maple syrup and remaining ingredients and combine with beans. Cover and bake for 4 hours. Uncover, add remaining maple syrup and bake another hour, adding water if necessary, at 325° or slow oven.

Pease

Mint Peas

Shell **fresh peas**. Put in **boiling water**, with a **small spring onion, a pinch of sugar, and salt**. Add a few **fresh mint leaves**. Simmer 8-10 minutes; do not overcook. Place in a serving bowl, top with **butter,** and serve.

Askin diary, 1774:

April 22 Sowed some pease at the farm

April 23 Mr Boyez Sewed Pease

May 6   Sowed Pease

May 10 Sowed the last Oats & Pease

May 28 Sowed Garden Pease

1775:

April 22 Sowed some Garden pease in my Gardin

April 29 Sowed Garden pease in drills 3 foot apart

May 6   Sowed Peas

May 8   Sowed Pease at the Farm

June 6   Sowed Pease to the 10th Inst

New Ground twice plowed

I think best for Pease [10]

PEASE PORRIDGE [11]

1 lb	split peas	2 T	butter
2	eggs		salt and pepper

Soak and cook split peas, drain liquid, and puree peas. Mash or use a food processor. Add butter, eggs, salt and pepper.

Pour into a greased bowl and cover with lid or foil. Seal tightly so it won't dry out. Steam for 1 hour. Place bowl on a trivet, in a Dutch oven. Place 2 inches of water in the bottom of the oven, cover tightly, and bake.

Leftovers can be sliced and fried in butter. This is traditionally served with pork and sausage.

CABBAGE

RED CABBAGE

1 head	cabbage, sliced	1 qt	water
2 T	butter	1/2	onion, chopped
pinch	grated nutmeg		

Place all ingredients in a pan, cover, and cook till cabbage is tender. Add **2 T vinegar** and **1 T brown sugar**. Simmer 5 minutes and serve hot.

Askin diary, 1774:

Nov 30th Took up my Cabbage out of my Garden

1775:

May 29th Transplanted Parsnip & some Cabbage plants three days Ago [12]

Notice that Askin "transplanted" cabbage plants. In northern Michigan, it is really necessary to start cabbage about 3-4 weeks ahead, in order to get a crop.

CABBAGE AND APPLES I
Choux aux Pommes

1 head	white cabbage, trimmed		
2 lbs	apples, unpeeled, sliced		
1 qt	salted water	5 strips	bacon, diced
$\frac{1}{2}$ tsp	salt	$\frac{1}{4}$ tsp	pepper
$\frac{1}{2}$ tsp	grated nutmeg		

Shred cabbage and blanch in salted water. Place alternate layers of apples and cabbage in a greased kettle. Fry bacon in another kettle and add it, with grease, to apple/cabbage mixture. Add seasonings, cover, and simmer 2 hours.

CABBAGE AND APPLES II

1 qt	salted water
1 head	cabbage, shredded
2	onions, finely chopped
2	apples, peeled, cored and cubed
1 T	butter
$\frac{1}{2}$ tsp	cinnamon
	salt and pepper

This is a similar recipe, with onions instead of bacon. It is fried and takes much less time to prepare.

Boil cabbage in salted water, covered, for 3 minutes. Drain and set aside. Fry onions and apples in butter until soft. Sprinkle with cinnamon. Add cabbage, warm over low heat for 2 minutes, and season. Serve warm.

BUBBLE AND SQUEAK

2 cups	leftover beef	1 sm	cabbage
1 T	vinegar		salt and pepper
1 cup	water		butter

Boil cabbage, drain, and chop into bite-size pieces. Add meat, water, and vinegar. Season to taste with salt, pepper and butter. Cook until warm. The escaping steam will "bubble and squeak" as the meal cooks.

COLCANNON

Traditionally served at Halloween in Scotland. Much like "bubble and squeak" except it adds potatoes and onions and is baked in an oven.

6	green onions (leeks)
²/₃ cup	milk
4 cups	mashed potatoes *(leftovers are fine)*
4 cups	cooked cabbage, chopped into small pieces
	salt and pepper
2 T	butter

Chop green onions finely and put in a pan with the milk. Cook just to the boiling point and set aside. Mix cabbage and potatoes. Add seasoning. Pour in milk and green onions; mix well. Bake 20 minutes. Top with butter.

CABBAGE WITH MILK

1 lg	cabbage, chopped coarsely		
¹/₂ cup	milk	2 T	butter
	salt and pepper		salted water

Bring a pan of salted water to boil and plunge cabbage in it for 2 minutes. Pour water off. Add milk and 1 T of the butter; season with salt and pepper. Simmer 15 minutes. Put into a serving dish, top with remaining butter, and serve warm.

Maple Sauerkraut

2 lbs	sauerkraut
1 sm	cabbage, shredded
2 sm	onions, chopped fine
1 cup	maple syrup

Cook sauerkraut and cabbage until fresh cabbage is wilted and tender. In a separate pan, saute onion until transparent. Add to sauerkraut mixture. Add maple syrup, mix, and cook slowly. Serve with sausage or as a side dish.

Sauerkraut

20 lbs	cabbage	½ lb	coarse salt

Shred cabbage. Layer with salt in a large ceramic crock, starting with cabbage and ending with salt. Cover with a clean cloth. Weight it down with a plate and a large rock. Keep it below 60° and above 40°. Remove the scum daily and replace with a clean cloth. Let stand at least a month. To can, heat to 180° and pack in hot jars. Seal and process. It can also be frozen in freezer bags. Makes 8 quarts.

Beets

Beets are hard to grow at Mackinac because of our large rabbit population. Early morning visitors often find a bunny having breakfast in one of the gardens. Perhaps the rabbits were not as bold in the 18th century or they would have ended up in a stew with the vegetables they found so tasty!

Askin diary, 1775:

Aprl 22d Harrowed the large Garden at the Fort

Tuesday May 2d Sowed Persley, Beets, Onions, Lettice & Barley Seeds[13]

PICKLED BEETS

2 cups	canned sliced beets (reserve juice)		
¹/₂ cup	vinegar	2 T	sugar
¹/₂ tsp	salt	dash	cloves
1 sm	bay leaf	1 sm	onion, sliced (optional)

In a pan, heat ¹/₄ cup of the reserved beet juice and all other ingredients. Bring to a boil. Reduce heat and simmer 5 minutes. Pour over beets. Refrigerate 1 hour until chilled.

A similar recipe adds 3 T cornstarch to thicken the sauce. Early cooks used to save corn silks, powder them, and use them to thicken sauces.

BEET TOPS

Beet tops can be eaten fresh. They are especially tasty when they are very small. Save **beet tops** when thinning young beets in the garden. Wash the sand off and place in a pan with **salted water**. Cover and cook until tender, 5-10 minutes. Drain. Serve with **melted butter**. Raw beet tops can also be added to salads.

Askin diary, 1775:

May 1st Sowed Turnip Seed in drills 2 foot apart with dung in the trench under the Seeds also parsnips

May 10th Sowed some More Lettice & carrott Seeds [14]

GARDEN VEGETABLES

CARROTS

We use the "early horn" carrot variety. This is traced back to the 1600s and came through the Dutch. It is an early carrot with a short blunt tip. It works especially well in the sandy Mackinac soil. We plant it every two weeks from Memorial weekend till mid-July. Carrots take 2-3 weeks to germinate so we plant them with radishes to help mark the row. By the time the carrots are ready to thin, the radishes are ready to pick. This helps keep people from walking on the carrots!

Carrots were eaten raw or cooked like potatoes. They were often added to soups and stews. They were usually stored in root cellars, underground. Sometimes carrots were just left in the garden during the winter and mulched with grass or straw. This could be removed and carrots pulled from the ground, if the snow wasn't too deep. This method tends to give a sweeter carrot. Another way of preserving was to cut them into thin slices and string them on a thread to dry. These strings were hung from the rafters, which helped keep the food away from the mice.

BAKED CARROT PUDDING

2 cups	grated carrots	1	onion, chopped
¼ tsp	salt	1 cup	water

Bring everything to a boil and cook 5 minutes. Mash or whip until smooth. Add the following ingredients:

1	egg, beaten	1 T	butter
½ cup	milk	¼ tsp	cinnamon
½ cup	dry bread crumbs		

Place in a crock and put on a trivet in a Dutch oven. Bake covered for 20 minutes.

PARSNIPS AND TURNIPS

Parsnips taste better when exposed to frost. They were often preserved by leaving them in the garden over the winter and digging up in the early spring. They were also stored in cellars in bins of sand. They were cooked, added to soups and stews, or boiled and mashed.

Wash and scrape or peel **parsnips or turnips**. Boil in **salted water** until soft. Drain and mash. Add **butter**. Serve and use like a mashed potato or mashed carrot.

Parsnips and turnips are prepared in a similar manner to carrots.

RADISHES

There were winter-keeping varieties of radishes as well as the more common red and white kind. These were large and some had a black skin. They were planted in August, harvested in October, then stored in underground root cellars. Peter Kalm mentioned "a radish which in the loose soil had grown so big as to be 7 inches in diameter." [15]

COOKED RADISHES

¹/₂ cup	diced onions	1 cup	sliced radishes
	butter		salt and pepper

Saute onions in butter. Add radishes and cook 10 minutes. Season.

CREAMED RADISHES

Steam **radishes** until tender. Place in a bowl and cover with a **white sauce**. Add some fresh dill leaf, if desired.

ONIONS

ONION/SALT PORK CASSEROLE[17]

Peel enough **onions** to fill a baking dish. Fry **1 cup diced salt pork**, until browned, and pour, with the fat, over the onions. Fill dish with boiling water about ¹/₃ full and place on a trivet inside a Dutch oven. Cover and steam for 1 hour. Remove cover and sprinkle with **bread crumbs**. Continue cooking another 30 minutes. Serve.

SKIRLIE

½ cup	oatmeal	1 lg	onion, sliced thinly
2 strips	bacon		salt and pepper

Chop bacon into 1-inch chunks and fry. When grease coats the pan, add sliced onion. Cook until transparent. Add oatmeal to absorb the fat, keeping the mixture thick. Stir for 7-10 minutes, till cooked. Serve with minced meat, roasted poultry, or as a main dish when the larder is bare.

In the 18th century, people did not worry about eating too much animal fat and cholesterol. Instead they tried to add fat to their diet, as it provided energy and helped keep the body warm.

Askin diary, 1774:

April 29th planted Onions for seed, also Beans Squash seed & Cucumbers

April 30th Sowed onion & spinage Seed

1775:

May 3rd Sowed More Garden Seeds & sett Shallotts & Beans [16]

SORREL

One of our favorite tricks to play on new staff members at Michilimackinac is to serve them lunch and have them try to identify what they are eating. One of our interpreters, Barb, is a master at locating edible weeds, indigenous to the area, and adding them to a salad. We often find her, with a basket, scouring the parade ground, the beach area, and especially the pile of weeds just pulled from the gardens. Using her past experience, and a good field guide, she can always be counted on to make a lunch out of nothing! We have tried to transplant samples of these plants into the herb garden so they are available for interpretation. Many a visitor has questioned our gardening ability when viewing the lush crop of dandelion greens, wild mustard, sorrel, and lamb's quarters growing next to the parsley, sage, rosemary, and thyme!

Sorrel, as well as lamb's quarters and dandelion greens, were used fresh in salads in the 18th century. They are washed and used like lettuce. These greens can also be gently boiled and used like spinach. Peter Kalm mentions they used vinegar to season it.

Askin diary, 1774:

April 19

   I sett the first potatoes

April 28th
   *sowed Parsnips & sett
   Potatoes at the farm
   also sowed Oates*

May 4th

   *Continued plowing &
   setting Potatoes*

May 11

   Sett the last potatoes

May 30th

   planted Potatoes

Nov 8th

   *Dug my Potatoes at the
   farm*

Nov 14th
   *Dug the last of my
   Potatoes* [18]

POTATOES

BAKED POTATO— ONION CASSEROLE

Fill a Dutch oven with layers of **sliced raw potatoes and onions**. Add **salt and pepper**. Add **milk** to cover potatoes. Top with **salt pork**. Bake, covered, at a low temperature until potatoes are tender and a crust forms (2-3 hours). This is a good dish to use when feeding a large number of people. Canned milk can be substituted for whole milk and used when camping or away from refrigeration.

SCOTS POTATO PIES
Early version of baked stuffed potatoes

potatoes	precooked meat
onion, parboiled	pepper
salt	gravy

Peel some large potatoes, nearly equal in size. Cut off the tops about $1/2$ inch and hollow out the center, leaving the potato at least $1/2$ inch thick all over. Mince some cooked scraps of meat, and mix with parboiled onion, salt and pepper, and moisten with gravy. Stuff potatoes with this mixture, put on the tops, and bake for at least an hour, basting occasionally with drippings.

   Serve with gravy (bouillon).

COLLOPS
Scalloped Potatoes

6	potatoes, washed and sliced thin		
2	onions, sliced thin	2 tsp	salt
3 T	butter	2 T	flour
	pepper	2¹/₂ cups	milk
2 T	chopped parsley		

Toss potatoes with flour and spices. Place in a Dutch oven. Add onions, butter, and milk. Cover and bake in coals until potatoes are tender, about 40 minutes. (Leftover meat, especially ham, can be added).

"Collops" or scallops was quickly adapted from the British Isles and soon became an everyday dish in North America. This dish calls for a milk or white sauce and is a little richer in fat. Other vegetables besides potatoes were also cooked in a white sauce, including scalloped onions, corn, and even radishes.

PRATIE OATEN
Irish Breakfast or Tea Dish

3 lg	potatoes	1 cup	rolled oats
¹/₂ cup	melted butter	1 tsp	salt
	bacon grease or shortening		

Boil potatoes in their skins. Peel, mash, and cool. (A wise cook would prepare some extra potatoes at a previous meal.)

Add oats, melted butter, and salt. Mix well. Roll out ¹/₂ inch thick. Cut into circles with a glass or biscuit cutter.

Heat bacon grease in a cast iron pan and fry until brown. Serve warm. (Makes 1 dozen.)

SQUASH

BAKED WINTER SQUASH

Bury a whole, uncut **squash** in the coals. Bake about an hour, testing with a fork for tenderness. Remove, cut it in half, and remove the seeds. Squash can be served in the shell (its own plate) or scooped out and placed in a serving bowl and topped with melted **butter, salt, and pepper.**

Or:

Cut **squash** in half and clean out the seeds. Place the cut sides back together; join with toothpicks. Bake in the ashes until squash is tender. Squash may be placed in a Dutch oven, open side up. Fill the cavity with **butter, salt, and pepper.** Place the lid on the kettle and bake in a slow bed of embers until squash is tender. Serve with **maple syrup or brown sugar.**

Or:

Cut **squash** in half and clean out the seeds. Bake, cut side down, with an inch of **water** in a covered pan. When tender, remove from pan and scoop out into a serving dish.

SUMMER SQUASH

Wash **squash**, peel, and cut in thin slices. Add **1 sliced onion** and **2 T butter**. Cook until soft and lightly browned. Add **salt, pepper, and herbs** to taste. Serve warm.

BAKED SQUASH PUDDING

$3^1/_2$ **cups frozen squash or cooked, mashed fresh squash**

1	egg	$^1/_3$ cup	milk
2 T	margarine	1 tsp	salt
$^1/_4$ tsp	pepper		

Combine ingredients and place in a crock. Place crock on a trivet in a Dutch oven. Bake on hot coals for 30 minutes.

WILD RICE

Wild rice was first washed and rinsed to remove dirt and chaff. It was simmered in water or broth until it absorbed moisture and became soft. When freshly harvested it can be cooked in about 10 minutes. Parched rice requires at least 30 minutes to soften. It was sometimes soaked overnight and allowed to swell before cooking. It was eaten as a side dish, used as a dressing with wild duck, used to thicken broths, and mostly added to stews and soups. Wild rice will triple in volume when cooked.

METHOD 1:
Cover the washed rice with boiling water and let it sit, covered, overnight. Drain and reheat in fresh water or add to a soup or casserole.

METHOD 2:
Cover with boiling water and allow to stand until cool. Drain. Repeat 3 times until the rice is tender.

METHOD 3:
When adding to soup, add early and be prepared to let it simmer a long time (like barley).

APPLES

We are attempting to replant an orchard at Michilimackinac with some early varieties. During the spring of 1995, twenty heritage apple varieties were planted outside the fort walls near the animal pens. There has been some difficulty in getting them established, as the rabbits, geese, and even some deer have stopped by to sample the young saplings. Once they start to produce fruit, this will be an exciting exhibit. The apples will not look like the standard Red Delicious and McIntosh varieties purchased in the grocery store today.

Madelaine Askin (John Askin, Jr's wife), from her home at St. Joseph Island, to her mother-in-law, Mrs John Askin Sr, in Detroit:

October 1807
I send you three or four apples in a small mocock [birch bark container]. They are from trees of which you planted the seeds at old Fort Mackinac, transplanted at the new fort on Dr. [David] Mitchell's place and were given to me by his daughter, Mrs. [Lewis] Crawford, who lives there now. [20]

Visitors will be able to sample apples of times past, and help to process some of them into apple butter, cider, and vinegar. We planted varieties that were used in the 18th century, are appropriate to the northern Michigan climate, and are still available today. Many old varieties are lost forever! Those planted at Michilimackinac include the Rhode Island Greening, Black Gilliflower, Snow Apple (Fameuse), Calville Blanc D'hiver, Baldwin, Newtown Pippen, Swayzie, Canada Red, Fall Russet, and Roxbury Russet.

APPLE SAUCE

½ gal	cider		3 lbs	apples
	sugar			butter
	cinnamon *(optional)*			

Simmer cider until reduced by half and very syrupy. Peel apples and cut into quarters. Stew apples in cider until soft. Add butter and sugar to taste. Makes 2 quarts.

   CAUTION: If preparing in brass kettles make sure the kettles are polished and delimed before beginning. The acid in the apples will remove all the tarnish from the pan and turn the applesauce a nice rusty brown.

BAKED APPLES

Use unblemished **apples**, one per serving. Remove the core and stem from each apple. Place in a shallow cake or pie pan. Season the opening with **butter, sugar, and cinnamon**, and fill with **raisins**, if desired. Pour an inch of water in the pan so the apples will not scorch or stick. Place pan in a Dutch oven and steam about 40 minutes, until tender.

Desserts

MAPLE SUGAR, as well as white refined sugar, was important to the diet at Michilimackinac. During the spring sap season, many Native Americans and French were involved in gathering and processing maple sugar. Sugar, molasses, brown sugar, and honey would be added to the flours and fruits of the area to produce some tasty treats. The British imported cane sugar from the West Indies. Chocolate was also imported in large amounts.

This chapter will be divided into four sections: cakes, pies, puddings, and other desserts. The recipes are all based on old ones that were popular in the 18th century.

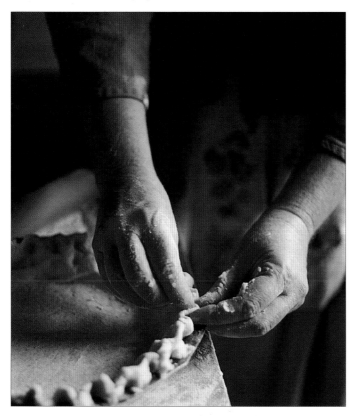

CAKES

Cakes of the 18th century were much heavier than today's spongy desserts. The flour was heavier and cakes didn't rise as high. Many of the old recipes call for a dozen eggs, beaten to a froth, to add leavening. Without the aid of an electric mixer the cook's arm must have had a workout! The cakes often were more highly seasoned than we would choose today—lots of cinnamon, nutmeg, and cloves. Also, they were dusted with sugar, but not frosted like today's version.

Two methods may be used to bake the cake. The easiest is to pour the batter into a preheated Dutch oven. Place the cover on, add hot coals to the lid, and bake until set. The other method is to pour the batter into a cake tin and place the tin on a trivet, inside a Dutch oven. This is preferable if the batter has a lot of sugar or fruit, as it helps keep the sugar from burning and the batter from sticking to the pan.

The modern cook can simply pour the batter into a greased and floured 9" x 12" cake pan and bake in an electric or gas oven the recommended time.

APPLESAUCE CAKE
Eggless

1 cup	brown sugar	1/3 cup	shortening
1 1/4 cups	applesauce	1 1/2 tsp	baking powder
1 tsp	baking soda	1 tsp	salt
2 cups	flour	1 tsp	cinnamon
1/2 tsp	cloves	1 cup	raisins

Beat shortening and sugar together. Sift dry ingredients and use some to dust the raisins. Mix dry ingredients into the sugar mixture alternately with the applesauce. Fold in raisins. Pour into a preheated Dutch oven, cover, and bake about 45 minutes.

DRIED APPLE CAKE

1½ cups	dried apples	½ cup	molasses
½ cup	butter	1 cup	sugar
2 cups	flour	1 cup	raisins or currants
1 cup	chopped nutmeats	½ cup	chopped dates
¼ tsp	salt	1 tsp	baking soda
1 tsp	nutmeg	½ tsp	cinnamon

Soak dried apples overnight. Drain and chop into small pieces. Add molasses and simmer until tender. Cool. Cream butter and sugar. In another bowl, combine dry ingredients. Slowly add dry ingredients to butter and sugar. Add apple/molasses mixture. Stir batter and pour into a pre-heated, greased Dutch oven. Cover and place coals on the lid. Bake about 1 hour. Add more coals as needed. Test with a straw; the cake is done when the straw comes out clean.

BLUEBERRY CAKE

4 cups	flour	1 cup	sugar
2 tsp	cream of tartar	½ tsp	salt
⅔ cup	butter	2	eggs, well beaten
1 cup	milk	1 tsp	baking soda
1½ cups	fresh blueberries (or huckleberries or wild strawberries)		

Sift flour, sugar, salt, and cream of tartar. Rub in butter. Add eggs. Add soda to milk and stir into batter. Gently fold in berries. Pour batter into a preheated Dutch oven and bake until the top is browned and springs back when touched.

BURNT SUGAR CAKE

SYRUP:

Melt $\frac{1}{2}$ **cup sugar** in a small pan, over low heat. Stir constantly, until dark-golden. Remove from heat and add $\frac{1}{2}$ **cup boiling water**. Cook over low heat until sugar is dissolved. Cool about 1 hour. Measure and add water to make 1 cup liquid.

BATTER:

$2\frac{1}{2}$ cups	flour	1 cup	white sugar
3 tsp	baking powder	1 tsp	salt
$\frac{1}{2}$ cup	shortening	2	eggs
1 tsp	vanilla extract		

Mix flour, sugar, baking powder, and salt. Add shortening and $\frac{3}{4}$ cup sugar syrup (above). Beat. Add eggs, vanilla, and remaining syrup. Beat until smooth. Pour into 2 greased and floured cake pans. Place pans on a trivet in a Dutch oven. Cover the lid with ashes and bake about 30 minutes, until the top is done. Remove from pans and cool on a towel or wire rack. Top with **powdered sugar**.

SOUR MILK CHOCOLATE CAKE

$\frac{1}{2}$ cup	cocoa	$2\frac{1}{4}$ cups	flour
$\frac{1}{2}$ tsp	baking soda	1 tsp	baking powder
$\frac{1}{2}$ tsp	salt	2 cups	sugar
2	eggs	1 cup	boiling water
1 tsp	vanilla	$\frac{1}{2}$ cup	soft butter
$\frac{1}{2}$ cup	sour milk		

To make sour milk add $1\frac{1}{2}$ tsp vinegar to whole milk

Mix dry ingredients in a small bowl. Beat liquid ingredients in a large bowl for 5 minutes. Add dry ingredients. Pour into a greased, floured 9" cake pan or Dutch oven and bake 30-35 minutes.

CHOCOLATE CAKE

1 cup	boiling water	2 squares	unsweetened chocolate
2 cups	flour	1/4 tsp	salt
1 tsp	baking soda	1/2 cup	soft butter
1 tsp	vanilla	1 3/4 cups	light brown sugar
2	eggs	1/2 cup	milk

Place boiling water and chocolate in a small bowl, until chocolate melts. In a second bowl, mix flour, salt, and soda. In a third bowl, beat butter, vanilla, sugar, and eggs until light and fluffy.

Add flour mixture to egg mixture, adding milk. Beat in chocolate mixture. Pour into a greased Dutch oven. Cover and bake about 1 hour.

SOURDOUGH CHOCOLATE CAKE

Let ferment for 2-3 hours until bubbly and there is a sour milk odor:

1/2 cup	thick sourdough starter *(see page 117)*		
1 cup	water	1/4 cup	dry milk
1 1/2 cups	flour		

Add:

1 cup	sugar	1/2 cup	shortening
1/2 tsp	salt	1 tsp	vanilla
1 1/2 tsp	baking soda	2	eggs
3 squares	melted chocolate		

Cream together sugar and shortening. Add salt, vanilla, and soda. Stir well and then beat in eggs. Add melted chocolate. Stir until blended. Gently fold sugar/egg mixture into sourdough mixture. Pour into a greased and floured cake pan. Set pan in the oven and bake at 350° for 25-30 minutes.

GINGERBREAD

1 cup	butter	1 cup + 2T	dark brown sugar
1¼ cups	molasses	2	eggs, beaten
2¼ cups	flour	2 tsp	ginger
1 T	cinnamon	3 T	warm milk
1 tsp	baking soda		

Melt butter, sugar, and molasses over low heat. Add eggs, flour, and spices and mix well. Add milk and soda. Pour into a greased Dutch oven. Cover and bake 40 minutes at 300°. Cut into squares and serve.

Molasses cake is similar to the Gingerbread above.

MOLASSES CAKE

1½ cups	flour	1½ tsp	baking soda
½ tsp	cinnamon	½ tsp	ginger
¼ tsp	cloves	¼ tsp	salt
1	egg, beaten	½ cup	melted butter
1 cup	light molasses	½ cup	hot water

Beat liquid ingredients in a large bowl. In a second bowl mix dry ingredients, add to liquid, and beat until smooth. Pour into a pan and bake 30-35 minutes at 375°.

OATCAKES

2 cups	rolled oats	¼ tsp	salt
¼ tsp	baking soda	6 T	hot water
1 T	bacon fat or margarine		

Mix 1⅓ cups of the oats with the salt and soda. Melt bacon fat. Add to dry ingredients. Stir in hot water to make a stiff dough. Sprinkle remaining oatmeal on the table. Turn dough onto table and knead thoroughly. Divide dough in halves. Roll in an 8-inch circle. Cut into 4 wedges. Cook on a preheated griddle—3 minutes on one side or until edges start to curl.

OATMEAL CAKE

½ cup	butter	1 cup	maple sugar
1 cup	white sugar	2	eggs
1½ cups	flour	1 tsp	baking powder
1 tsp	baking soda	1 tsp	salt
2 tsp	cinnamon	1 tsp	nutmeg
1 tsp	vanilla	1½ cups	boiling water
1 cup	oatmeal		

Let oatmeal and boiling water soak 20 minutes. Cream butter and sugars together. Add eggs; beat well. Add oatmeal. Add dry ingredients. (Add raisins, nuts, if desired.) Pour into a Dutch oven, and bake until top springs back.

OATMEAL CAKES [2]

1 cup	shortening	1 cup	sugar
2	eggs	1/2 cup	molasses
1/4 cup	milk	2 cups	flour
1/2 tsp	salt	1/2 tsp	baking soda
2 tsp	cinnamon	1 tsp	cloves
2 cups	oats	1/2 cup	raisins

Mix dry ingredients in a medium bowl. In a large bowl, cream sugar and shortening until smooth. Add eggs, molasses, and milk. Add dry ingredients slowly and mix well.

Roll out on a floured board and cut into circles using a cup or cookie cutter. Place on a baking sheet and bake until lightly browned, about 8-10 minutes.

This recipe works well if you have a tin reflector oven. We have baked them, 5 at a time, in a covered Dutch oven.

QUEEN'S CAKE [3]
Named for Queen Charlotte, who was the wife of King George III

Pour **1 cup boiling water** over **1 cup chopped dates** and **1 tsp baking soda** and let stand.

2 cups	sugar	1/2 cup	butter
2	eggs, beaten	2 tsp	vanilla
3 cups	sifted flour	2 tsp	baking soda
2/3 tsp	salt		

Cream together sugar and butter. Add beaten eggs and vanilla. In a second bowl, sift flour, soda, and salt together. Add dry ingredients to wet 1/3 at a time. Fold in dates. Pour into a greased Dutch oven, cover, and bake about 35 minutes. Top with a boiled sauce made from **5 T brown sugar, 5 T heavy cream** and **2 T butter**.

POUND CAKE

2 cups	flour	2 tsp	baking powder
1½ cups	sugar	¾ cup	butter
3	eggs	½ tsp	vanilla
	caraway seed or currants *(optional)*		

Cream sugar and butter. Add eggs and vanilla. Stir in flour and baking powder. Add caraway or currants if desired. Pour into a greased pan and bake until firm. This cake may be made ahead and stored, as its flavor improves with age.

Old recipes called for a pound of butter, a pound of eggs, a pound of sugar and a pound of flour. Some recipes called for rosewater.

MACKINAC TRIFLE

Prepare a cake like the **pound cake** or an angel food cake. Break it into pieces and place in a large glass bowl. Drizzle a **glass of wine** over the cake and then pour a **custard** *(see page 155)* over it. Garnish with fresh **berries** and **whipped cream**.

ROSEWATER-CURRANT CAKE

1 cup	soft unsalted butter	1½ cups	sugar
5	eggs	2 cups	sifted white flour
2 T	rosewater	1 tsp	vanilla
¾ cup	dried currants or raisins		

Cream butter and sugar. Add eggs, beating well. Slowly mix in flour, adding ½ cup at a time. Add rosewater and vanilla and mix well. Fold in currants.

    Pour into a greased and floured cake pan. Place on a trivet in a Dutch oven and bake 1½ hours at 300° until a toothpick inserted comes out clean. Remove from the pan and cool on a rack.

Rosewater was used much like we use vanilla today. It is available in Middle East foreign food sections of the grocery store. Try it sparingly until you determine if you like the taste. You may want to use half rosewater and half vanilla.

SUGAR CAKES
Cookies

1 cup	sugar	1/4 cup	shortening
4 T	butter	1	egg
1/4 cup	milk	1 tsp	vanilla
2 cups	flour	1 tsp	baking soda
1/4 tsp	salt	2 tsp	cream of tartar

Sift dry ingredients and set aside. In a second bowl, cream butter, sugar, and shortening. Add vanilla, egg, and milk. Add dry ingredients. Form into 1-inch balls, roll in white sugar, and place on ungreased cookie sheet. Flatten with a glass and bake at 350° for 10 minutes, until lightly browned.

SPICE CAKE I
Eggless

1 cup	brown sugar	1/2 cup	shortening
2 1/2 cups	flour	1 tsp	salt
1 tsp	cinnamon	1 tsp	cloves
1/2 tsp	nutmeg	1 1/4 tsp	baking soda
1 cup	sour milk	1/2 cup	raisins
1/2 cup	chopped nutmeats		

During the winter eggs would be scarce. This spice cake, made without eggs, might have been prepared for one of the weekly winter dance parties.

Cream shortening and sugar in a large bowl. Sift flour, soda, and spices in a second bowl, mixing spices in thoroughly. Dust the raisins with a little of the flour. Add milk and dry ingredients alternately to the sugar. Fold in raisins and nuts. Pour into a greased Dutch oven, cover, and bake till top springs back when touched. Remove from pan and cool on rack or towel.

SPICE CAKE II
with Eggs

3 cups	flour	1 T	cinnamon
1 T	cloves	1 tsp	baking powder
½ tsp	baking soda	⅛ tsp	salt
1 cup	raisins or currants	1 cup	soft butter
1 cup	brown sugar	1¼ cups	white sugar
5	eggs	1 cup	sour milk

To sour milk: Add 1 T vinegar and let stand 5 minutes.

Coat raisins with flour. Mix dry ingredients and set aside. Mix butter and sugar, beating until light and fluffy. Add flour mixture to wet ingredients. Pour into a greased Dutch oven, cover, and bake 50 minutes at 350°.

CUSTARD

2 cups	cream	2 cups	milk
¾ cup	sugar	6	eggs, well beaten
	fresh grated nutmeg		

Combine cream, milk, and sugar. Heat over warm coal, stirring constantly, until mixture reaches the boiling point. Remove from fire. Pour about ½ cup of the hot liquid into the eggs, stirring constantly, with a whisk. Pour eggs into remaining liquid, stirring constantly. Return to heat and continue to stir until mixture thickens. Pour into a bowl and set in a windowsill to cool. Sprinkle nutmeg over custard when served.

PIES

Pie crusts were known as coffins or pastes. They were usually very simple, with flour, water, and lard. Some had a cakier texture and a few more ingredients. Some of the meat pie crusts were more like a biscuit and were single top crusts. To bake a pie, form the crust and filling in the usual way. Place the pie tin on a trivet in a Dutch oven. Cover with the lid and surround the pan and lid with hot coals. Replenish as necessary. Check the pie occasionally and remove and set on a rack when done. Be careful when removing the pie tin from the oven. They are a tight fit and the hot juice can pour over the edge and burn the cook's fingers.

PIE CRUST WITH LARD

This makes enough for a double crust pie.

2 cups	flour	1¼ tsp	salt
⅔ cup	lard	6-7 T	cold water

In a large bowl, combine flour with salt. Cut lard into flour until it resembles coarse gravel. Add enough water to moisten and stir until it starts to form a ball.

Sprinkle a cutting board with flour and roll the dough into 2 circles. Place one in a pie pan, fill, and cover with the top crust. Cut slits in the top and bake.

No Fail Pie Crust
This makes enough for 2 double crust pies.

3 cups	sifted flour	1 tsp	baking powder
1 tsp	salt	1¼ cups	lard
1	egg	6 T	water
1 T	vinegar		

Sift flour, baking powder, and salt. Cut in lard. Beat egg, water, and vinegar. Sprinkle over flour mixture, tossing lightly until dough is moist enough to hold together.

This pastry has a cakey texture.

Apple Pie Filling

6 med	apples, peeled, cored and sliced
double	pie crust *(see page 156)*

Mix together:

1 cup	sugar	1 tsp	cinnamon
4 T	flour	dash	salt

Coat apples with sugar mixture and place in a pie crust. Dot with butter. Cover with a top crust which may be sprinkled with sugar. Cut a design in top crust, to allow steam to escape. Bake at 375° for 45 minutes.

Dried Apple Pie

1½ cups	dried apple		
single	pie crust *(see page 156)*		
1 cup	cider	1 tsp	cinnamon
1 cup	applejack or whiskey	1 cup	brown sugar
	ginger and nutmeg to taste		

Soak dried apples overnight in cider and whiskey (or just 2 cups cider). Simmer till fruit softens. Add sugar and spices. Pour into prepared pie crust, dot with butter, and bake about 45 minutes.

SQUASH OR PUMPKIN PIE

1 sm	pumpkin or other winter squash		
2	eggs	2 cups	milk
¹/₂ cup	molasses	dash	salt
2 T	cinnamon	1 T	ginger
single	pie crust *(see page 156)*		

Cut up pumpkin, remove seeds, and pare outside rind. Simmer in a covered pan in a small amount of water until tender. Drain water and discard. Force pumpkin through a sieve. Measure 2 cups puree for each pie. Remainder may be frozen or dried.

Beat eggs and add milk. When blended, add pumpkin, molasses, salt, cinnamon, and ginger and stir well. Pour into pie crust in a 9" pie plate. Bake at 400° for 15 minutes and then at 375° for 30 minutes or longer, until set.

GOOSEBERRY PIE

double	pie crust *(see page 156)*		
4 cups	fresh gooseberries		
5 T	flour	1¹/₂ cups sugar	

Snip off the stem and blossom ends of berries. Wash and drain. In a bowl, mix together sugar and flour. Fold in berries. Line a pie pan with crust, spoon in gooseberry mixture, and cover with a top crust. Vent to allow steam to escape. Place pie pan on a trivet, inside a Dutch oven, cover, and bake about 40 minutes. Replace the coals on the lid and around the oven as necessary, using a fairly hot fire.

Wild gooseberries used to be available in Northern Michigan. During the lumbering era they were torn out as they sometimes harbor a pine tree blister rust blight. Disease-resistant varieties from Europe have been reintroduced and now are available in Michigan nurseries. They should still be planted 300 feet away from pine trees.

Canned gooseberries are available in larger grocery stores in gourmet fruit sections.

BERRY PIE I
Simple

4 cups	fresh berries	1 T	lemon juice *(optional)*
1 cup	sugar	1/4 cup	flour
2 T	butter	double	pie crust *(see page 156)*

Clean berries and place in a bowl. Add sugar and lemon juice. Sprinkle flour on berries. Pour into pie crust, and dot with butter. Cover with top crust. Cut slits to allow steam to escape. Bake until browned.

BERRY PIE II
Thicker and Spicier

4 cups berries (strawberries, raspberries, blackberries, huckleberries)

Add :

1 cup	white sugar	1/4 cup	flour
2 T	butter	2 T	brown sugar
1/4 t	salt	1/4 t	nutmeg
1/4 t	cloves	double	pie crust *(see page 156)*
1 T	tapioca *or*	2 T	cornstarch

Clean berries and place in a bowl. Add sugars, flour, salt, and spices. Sprinkle tapioca or cornstarch on berries for thickening. Pour into pie crust, and dot with butter. Cover with top crust. Cut slits to allow steam to escape. Bake until browned.

*Little Jack Horner sat in
a corner
Eating a Christmas pie,
He put in a thumb,
And pulled out a plum,
And said "What a good
boy am I."*

PLUM PIE

4 cups	fresh plums	1 cup	sugar
¼ cup	flour	¼ tsp	salt
1 T	butter	single	pie crust *(see page 156)*

Wash, stone, and dice plums. Place in the bottom of a pie plate. Combine flour, sugar, and salt. Sprinkle over plums. Dot with butter. Prepare top pie crust. Roll out. Moisten the top edge of pie plate with water. Seal top crust and cut a slit to allow steam to escape. (And to allow space to "put in a thumb and pull out a plum"!) Bake until crust is browned.

RHUBARB PIE

Rhubarb was most commonly used as a medicinal herb during the 18th century. Recipes were just starting to call for it in baking pies and stewing fruits.

single	pie crust *(see page 156)*		
8 cups	rhubarb, cut in 1-inch pieces		
¼ tsp	ground cloves	1 tsp	cinnamon
1³⁄₄ cups	brown sugar *or*		
1 cup	white sugar *and*	³⁄₄ cup	brown sugar

Combine rhubarb, sugar, and spices. Simmer 1 hour, until tender. Use low heat so sugar does not burn. Prepare crust and fill. Bake in a Dutch oven 40 minutes.

MOLASSES PIE

3	eggs	1 cup	brown sugar
1 cup	molasses	1/2 tsp	salt
1/4 cup	melted butter	1 cup	chopped nuts
1 tsp	vanilla	single	pie crust *(see page 156)*

Beat eggs, sugar, molasses, salt, and butter together. Cook until sugar is dissolved and mixture is syrupy. Add nuts and vanilla. Pour into prepared pie crust. Place on a trivet in a Dutch oven. Cover, place coals on the lid, and bake until set and crust is browned, about 45 minutes.

SUGAR PIE

1 cup	milk	1 cup	brown sugar
3 T	flour	pinch	salt
single	pie crust *(see page 156)*		

Mix ingredients and beat well. Pour into prepared pie crust and place on a trivet in a Dutch oven. Bake, with coals under and on top of the oven, until custard is set.

This sugar pie is similar to the molasses pie, except for the use of milk instead of eggs to make the filling.

MAPLE SUGAR PIE

1 1/2 cups	maple syrup	1/2 tsp	baking soda
1 cup	flour	1 cup	brown sugar
1/2 cup	butter	single	pie crust *(see page 156)*

Heat maple syrup with soda until dissolved. Do not let it boil. Cool and pour into prepared pie crust. Combine flour, brown sugar, and butter in a bowl. Pour over the top of the maple syrup. Bake the pie 30 minutes at medium heat (350°).

It is a good idea to line the oven with foil because the sugar sometimes boils over and makes a sticky mess.

PUDDINGS

In the 17th century puddings were traditionally placed in a cloth bag or animal gut and boiled right in the soup kettle, along with the rest of the meal. By the 18th century it was more common to place the pudding in a bowl or tin and bake it in a side oven or steam it in a Dutch oven. Since Michilimackinac's fireplaces were small and did not include side ovens, we bake pudding in a Dutch oven. The bowl or crock of pudding is placed on a trivet and placed inside a preheated Dutch oven. An inch or two of water under the trivet will help steam it. It must be kept covered to retain the steam. A pudding can be browned by passing a "salamander" over it. This is a flat iron with a long handle. When heated in the fireplace, and then held over food closely, it will toast the surface.

Pudding bags were large squares of well washed linen or closeweave cotton. The "puddin" cloth was dipped in boiling hot water, wrung out, and then floured on one side. This flour would seal the fabric and create a barrier between the pudding and the boiling water. To use a pudding cloth, place it flour side up, in a clean bowl. Pour the batter into it, bring the cloth edges together, and tie them loosely, leaving room for the batter to rise or expand. Lift the pudding bag carefully and drop it into a kettle of boiling water. The bag should float freely, with the water level reaching the middle of the bag.

To prepare puddings in a modern kitchen, the cook can bake them in the oven. The pudding bowl or mold should be placed in a larger pan with an inch or two of water in the bottom. This will create a double boiler and steam the pudding so it doesn't burn.

Many of the puddings were served with a sauce over the top. One of the simplest was the following milk sauce.

MILK SAUCE

1 cup	milk	⅓ cup	brown sugar
1 tsp	vanilla	dash	nutmeg

Stir together and serve chilled, over pudding.

RUM SAUCE

1 cup	sugar	¼ cup	butter
2	eggs, separated	1 T	dark rum

Cream butter and sugar together. Place in a saucepan and add beaten egg yolks. Cook slowly until mixture coats the back of a wooden spoon. Beat egg whites and fold into the sauce. Add rum and serve hot, over pudding.

WINE SAUCE

½ cup	brown sugar	½ cup	water
1 T	butter	2 tsp	cornstarch
½ cup	port or Madeira wine		
dash	nutmeg		

Bring brown sugar and water to a boil. Cream together butter and cornstarch. Add to syrup. Stir and add wine, and nutmeg. Heat almost to boiling and serve over pudding.

STEAMED APPLE PUDDING

1½ cups	sifted flour	1 tsp	baking soda
½ tsp	salt	½ tsp	cinnamon
½ tsp	nutmeg	¼ tsp	cloves
¼ cup	butter	1 cup	sugar
2	eggs, well beaten	½ cup	raisins
4	cooking apples, sliced very thin		

Sift flour, soda, salt, and spices. In a large bowl, cream butter, sugar, and eggs until smooth and light. Stir in apples and raisins. Stir flour mixture into fruit mixture. Pour into a greased crock. Place crock on a trivet, in a large kettle. Pour boiling water into kettle to act as a steamer. Cover and bring to a boil. Simmer gently, 2 hours. Remove from heat; let stand until cool enough to remove. Tip onto a plate and serve.

ANOTHER APPLE PUDDING

4	apples, cored, peeled, and chopped		
1 tsp	baking soda	1 cup	light molasses
2½ cups	flour	pinch	salt
½ cup	water		

Add soda to molasses. Stir and mix with flour and salt. Add apples. Add water to thin the batter. Put in a crock and place on a trivet in a Dutch oven. Place 2 inches of water in the bottom of the oven so as to create steam. Leave the lid on during cooking and bake until set, about 2 hours.

APPLE/BREAD PUDDING

Line a Dutch oven with **slices of bread** that have been dipped in **milk**. Lay **6 sliced, cored apples** on top. Sprinkle with **¼ cup sugar, 1 tsp cinnamon, and dash of nutmeg.** Cover with more slices of bread, soaked in milk. Cover and bake 1 hour with low heat.

BREAD PUDDING

2 cups	dry bread crumbs *(Use as much bread as the pan will hold.)*		
1 cup	milk	1 cup	sugar
¼ cup	shortening	⅓ cup	raisins
1 T	cinnamon	½ tsp	cloves
½ tsp	allspice	1 T	baking soda
½ cup	nuts		
2 T	molasses *(optional)*		

Mix all ingredients and place in a baking casserole. Place on a trivet in a Dutch oven. Bake until browned.

BOILED BREAD PUDDING

1 loaf	bread	4 cups	milk, scalded
5	eggs	1/4 tsp	salt
1/2 cup	sugar		

Cut crusts off bread and cut in cubes. Place in a large bowl.
Cover with scalded milk and let it soak 1 hour. Beat eggs and
pour over bread. Add sugar and salt.

Dip a pudding cloth in cold water, sprinkle one side with
flour, and place it in a bowl. Pour pudding into it and tie
tightly. Drop into boiling water and let boil 2 hours. Remove
from water, untie, and turn into serving bowl. Spoon a sauce,
fruit, or preserves over the top and serve.

BRANDY SAUCE
for Bread Pudding

2 T	butter	2 T	brandy
1 cup	sugar	1 tsp	flour

Melt butter and add brandy. Mix sugar and flour and add to
brandy mixture. Stir until thick.

MAPLE BREAD PUDDING

3/4 cup   maple syrup
3 slices buttered bread, cut in cubes
2   eggs, beaten   2 cups   milk

Grease a crock. Put syrup in the bottom. Place bread as a second layer. Beat eggs in a bowl, add milk, and pour over bread. Do not mix layers. Place on a trivet in a Dutch oven. Add water to the bottom of the pan to steam. Cover and bake until set, about $1\frac{1}{2}$ hours. Dish up pudding and top with the sauce that formed in bottom of pan.

BLUEBERRY PUDDING

2 cups   blueberries or huckleberries
5   eggs   4 cups   milk
3 T   butter   pinch   salt
6 T   sugar   flour

Clean berries and roll in flour. Beat eggs, add milk and butter. Add berries, salt, and sugar. Pour into a crock. Place on a trivet in a Dutch oven. Cover and bake at low heat until pudding is set.

CARROT PUDDING

3 cups	cooked, mashed carrots		
4 T	sugar	3	eggs yolks
1½ T	cornstarch	1 cup	milk
1 cup	bread crumbs	2 T	butter
1 tsp	salt	½ tsp	nutmeg
1 cup	cream		

Beat egg yolks and sugar. Mix cornstarch with 2 T of the milk, until dissolved. Heat remaining milk, add cornstarch, and cook until thick. While stirring constantly, whip in egg yolk mixture. Cook till thick. Add carrots, bread crumbs, butter, and salt. Stir in cream. Add nutmeg. Pour into a crock, place on a trivet in a Dutch oven, and steam until set, about 1 hour.

COTTAGE PUDDING
An early version of upside-down cake

A similar version of this recipe called for sliced apples and cranberries to line the baking dish. Cinnamon and nutmeg were added to the batter, which was placed on top of the fruit and baked.

1 cup	flour	2 tsp	baking powder
¼ tsp	salt	1 T	butter
½ cup	sugar	1	egg
½ cup	milk		
	chopped fruit, raisins, or jam		

Line the bottom of a cake pan or crock with fruit. In a bowl, combine flour, baking powder, and salt. In a second bowl, cream butter, sugar, and egg. Add flour mixture and milk. Place in the pan on top of the fruit. Place pan on a trivet in a Dutch oven, and bake about 30 minutes, until done. Serve warm. Delicious topped with cream.

CUSTARD

1½ cups	milk	2 tsp	cornstarch
1 T	sugar	3	egg yolks
½ tsp	vanilla		

Mix cornstarch with 2 T of the milk. Add remaining milk and sugar. Heat until sauce begins to thicken and come to a boil. In a bowl, beat egg yolks. Slowly beat in a cup of the sauce, beating as you pour. Add mixture to pan, stirring well, and bring to a boil. Add vanilla. Pour into a dish and serve.

FIGGY PUDDING

2 cups	chopped, dried figs		
2 cups	bread crumbs	1 cup	flour
½ cup	sugar	1 tsp	salt
2 tsp	baking powder	2 eggs,	beaten
	milk		

Combine dry ingredients and stir well. Add eggs and enough milk to moisten well. Pour into a greased crock. Place crock on a trivet in a Dutch oven. Put water in the bottom of the oven to create steam. Bake about 2 hours, adding more water if necessary. Serve with a hard sauce, below.

HARD SAUCE:

½ lb	unsalted butter	¾ cup	dark brown sugar
5 T	rum or brandy	¼ tsp	nutmeg

Cream butter and sugar until smooth. Stir in brandy or rum. Add nutmeg. Beat thoroughly and set in a covered dish. Allow to harden before serving. No cooking required!

King George I was known as "Pudding George" and is the Georgie Porgie in the nursery rhyme:

Georgie Porgie, pudding pie,
Kissed the girls and made them cry [5]

INDIAN PUDDING

4 cups	milk	1/3 cup	cornmeal
1 cup	light molasses	1/4 cup	butter
1 tsp	salt	1/2 tsp	cinnamon
1	egg, beaten	1/2 cup	raisins

Boil milk in a double boiler, formed from placing a crock inside a kettle of boiling water. Stir corn meal into milk. Cook 20 minutes with water at full boil. Add molasses and cook 5 more minutes. Remove from the fire. Add butter, salt, cinnamon, raisins, and egg, stirring constantly.

Grease a baking crock or bowl and pour batter in. Place a trivet in the kettle, leaving an inch of water in the bottom. Place the crock on the trivet, cover, and steam for 1 hour.

MARLBOROUGH PUDDING[6]

This recipe was used as early as the 1600s.

3/4 cup	applesauce	3/4 cup	sugar
3/4 cup	white wine	6 T	melted butter
4	eggs, beaten		
	juice and grated rind of 1 lemon		
1 cup	milk	1/2	nutmeg, grated

Combine applesauce, sugar, wine, and butter. Stir in eggs, lemon, and milk. Pour into a greased crock. Grate nutmeg over the pudding. Place crock on a trivet in a Dutch oven and bake until set. Serve warm with **maple syrup**.

Rice Pudding

½ cup	raw white rice	3 cups	milk
pinch	salt	5 T	sugar
½ tsp	vanilla	1 T	butter
½ tsp	grated nutmeg		

Butter a crock and place rice in the bottom. In a pan, heat milk, salt, sugar, and vanilla. Stir until it begins to simmer. Pour over rice, dot with butter, and sprinkle nutmeg on top.

Place crock on a trivet in a Dutch oven. Place the lid on top and cover with coals. Bake at a low temperature for 2 hours, until rice is soft and pudding is creamy.

Roly-Poly Pudding
Jelly Roll, traditionally a boiled pudding

1 cup	flour	1 tsp	baking powder
1 tsp	cinnamon	¼ tsp	salt
¼ cup	shredded suet	6-8 T	water
4 T	warm jam		

Sift dry ingredients. Stir in suet. Add enough water to make a soft dough. Turn onto a lightly floured board and roll into a rectangle. Spread with warm jam. Fold up jelly-roll style. This may be placed in a floured bag and treated as a boiled pudding. It may also be baked like a cake.

SUET PUDDING

Make sour milk by adding 1 T vinegar to whole milk.

1 cup	chopped beef suet	1 cup	chopped dates
$2/3$ cup	molasses	1 cup	sour milk
1 tsp	baking soda	1 tsp	cinnamon
1 tsp	baking powder	$1/2$ tsp	ground cloves
$1/2$ tsp	salt	1 cup	nutmeats
1-3 cups flour			

Mix suet and dates. Set aside. In a large mixing bowl, combine sour milk and molasses. Add suet mixture. Add soda, powder, and spices. Stir in flour, $1/2$ cup at a time, until a stiff batter is formed. (The amount of flour varies because of the suet.) Add nutmeats. Pour batter into a crock and place in a Dutch oven. Add water to oven to create steam. Bake at low heat $2^1/_2$ hours, until pudding is firmly set.

If baking in a modern oven, place batter in an oven-proof dish. Set that pan within a larger pan. Add water to larger pan to create steam. Bake at 300° for $2^1/_2$ hours.

OTHER DESSERTS

This last selection of desserts uses a variety of baking methods.

Each artifact has a story to tell about the people of Michilimackinac. Broken tea cups speak of their long journey from China where they were made. The also tell about the popularity of tea at this frontier outpost.

APPLE PAN DOWDY
Brown Betty or Apple Crisp

Place the following in a crock:

4 cups	sliced apples	¼ cup	cold water
1 tsp	cinnamon	1 tsp	salt

TOPPING:

1 cup	sugar	⅓ cup	butter
1 cup	flour		

Cream butter and sugar; add flour and mix lightly with a fork. Sprinkle the topping on the apple mixture. Place crock on a trivet in a Dutch oven. Cover with lid and embers. Bake for 30 minutes. A modern cook can place it in a casserole and bake uncovered at 300° for 30 minutes.

APPLE DUMPLINGS

6	baking apples	6 T	white sugar
½ tsp	nutmeg	½ tsp	cinnamon
6 T	butter	double	pie crust

SYRUP:
2 cups light brown sugar and **1 cup water**, gently boiled 5 minutes.

Core apples. Mix sugar and spices. Roll crust into 6 circles. Place an apple in the center of each pastry circle. Fill the center of each apple with 1T butter and 1T spice/sugar mixture. Wrap dough around each apple and seal. Place dumplings on a pie tin. Put tin on a trivet in a Dutch oven and bake 30 minutes. Remove from oven, place dumplings in a serving bowl, and spoon syrup on top.

Peter Kalm, 1748:

One apple dish which the English prepare is as follows: take an apple and pare it, make a dough of water, flour and butter. Roll it thin and enclose apple in it. This is then bound in a clean linen cloth, put in a pot and boiled. When done it is taken out, placed on table and served. While it is warm, the crust is cut on one side. Thereupon they mix butter and sugar, which is added to the apples; then the dish is ready. They call this apple dumpling, sometime apple pudding.[7]

GOOSEBERRY FOOL

1 lb	gooseberries	2T	butter
3 T	sugar	1½ cups	heavy cream

Pinch the ends off the gooseberries. Melt butter in a pan and add gooseberries and sugar. Cover and cook over low heat, until soft and mushy. Mash berries and pass through a sieve. Discard the skins. Taste and add more sugar, if it's too tart. Set aside to cool. Whip cream and fold into gooseberry pulp. Spoon into custard cups and chill before serving. (Raspberries, strawberries or huckleberries may be substituted.)

BLUEBERRY FLUMMERY

1 quart	blueberries (or berries in season)		
2 cups	water	1 cup	sugar
pinch	salt		butter
8 slices	white bread		cream

Stew berries with water, sugar, and salt for 15 minutes. Butter bread slices. Place layers of bread and berries in a buttered crock. Place crock on a trivet in a Dutch oven and bake about 20 minutes. Remove crock and let cool. Serve in a bowl with cream.

PORT JELLY

2½ cups	port wine	1 envelope	unflavored gelatin
2 tsp	lemon juice	½ cup	sugar
¼ t	nutmeg	½ t	cinnamon

Soak gelatin in ½ cup of the port, until dissolved. Stir in 1 cup port with lemon and sugar. Add nutmeg and cinnamon and bring to a boil over low heat, stirring constantly. Stir in remaining port, pour into serving glasses, and allow to set until hardened, about 2 hours.

MADEIRA WINE JELLY

4 envelopes	unflavored gelatin		
½ cup	cold water	2 cups	grape juice
2 cups	Madeira wine	6 T	lemon juice
pinch	salt	1 cup	sugar

Dissolve gelatin in cold water. In a saucepan, boil grape juice. Add gelatin. Stir in Madeira, lemon juice, and salt. Add sugar to taste. Pour into mold or bowl to set. Chill till firm. Garnish with frosted fruit. Use fresh berries which have been dipped in egg white and rolled in granulated sugar. These need to be prepared the day before and dried at room temperature.

Gelatins were made from "calf's foot" broth boiled to a gelatin-like consistency. During the 18th century isinglass was also used. This was made from the bladder of fish.

BEVERAGES

RUM WAS A MAJOR item of the fur trade and came through Mackinac by the barrel. Finer wines were used by the upper class traders and officers. The common soldier probably had to make do with his small daily ration of rum and perhaps some spruce beer, which was drunk to prevent scurvy. Milk was not the common daily beverage it is today. The lack of pasteurization and refrigeration meant it would spoil easily and could make you sick. Milk was processed into cheese and butter rather than used as a beverage.

It is not clear how common it was to drink water. In those days the Great Lakes were not polluted and people here were surrounded with the largest source of fresh water in the world. However, those coming from England and France would have been so accustomed to avoiding drinking water that they may have continued to do so here. In Europe it was common for raw sewage to be dumped in the streets, and after a rain it all ran into the rivers. Those rivers were the water supplies for cooking, laundry, and cleaning. When people drank unboiled water from these rivers, they caught a multitude of fevers and diseases. Through time, they learned that the fermentation process (alcohol formation) of wine, cider, and beer made these beverages much healthier to drink than water.

From medieval times, English people had come to rely on beverages such as cider, beer, and wine. When these people emigrated to America, they brought this custom with them. Coffee, wines, and teas were expensive. Cider provided a tasty, safe, cheap beverage that could often be made at home. A great quantity of apples was processed into cider. The cider was placed in barrels and then shipped and stored till needed. A new batch of cider was expected to last until the next crop of apples was in. A major use of cider was as a pickling

Alcoholic beverages mentioned in Askin's inventories and letters included:

Cherry brandy

Rum

Shrub (brandy or rum, with sugar and spices, poured over fruit)

Mallaga (a dark dessert wine from Malaga, Spain)

Porter (a strong red wine from Portugal)

Red wine

British brandy

French brandy

W. Indie rum

Madeira (an amber tinted wine made of white grapes from the island of Madeira)

Ayle

agent. Before the days of refrigeration and freezers, pickling was a common method of food preservation. Apple cider could be fermented to vinegar and used to preserve meats, fruits and vegetables. Some cider was distilled into brandy (Apple Jack) and used as an antiseptic, anesthetic and sedative for medicinal purposes.

There are several steps in cider making. The first step is to crush the apples to a pulp. Next the pulp has to stand, exposed to the air, in order to sweeten and produce good color. (A problem in colonial days was to keep the flies away during this process!) The pulp was then shaped into cakes called "cheeses" and pressed. The juice was collected and put in a new barrel. Next the cider would ferment and bubble. If exposed to air at this stage, it would turn to vinegar. The barrels had to be topped off frequently and when the fermenting stopped, the bung holes were sealed tightly and the liquid allowed to settle. Next, in a process called "racking," the clear upper fluid was siphoned off into clean barrels, leaving the sediment in the bottom of the old. Sometimes a strip of sulphured rag was burned in the barrel to kill the bacteria that caused cider to sour. The complete process could take months and is similar to making wine.

Glass bottles from England, excavated at Michilimackinac, reveal the thirst for alcohol and the trans-Atlantic crossing that brought the bottles to the Straits of Mackinac.

MULLED CIDER

½ gal	fresh cider	½ tsp	nutmeg
1 stick	cinnamon	6	whole cloves
1	apple, orange or lemon		

Heat cider in a kettle. If using a copper kettle, remove all tarnish first or it will end up in the cider! Add cinnamon stick. Stick the cloves in the fruit, which will float on top. Stir in nutmeg and simmer by the fire. Spices may also be tied into a cheesecloth sack and floated in the cider.

HOT TODDY

12	apples	1 qt	brandy
2 T	brown sugar	2 T	ground ginger
6	whole cloves	1 T	ground cinnamon
dash	nutmeg	6 cups	boiling water

Core 6 apples and bake until the skins burst. Remove skins and mash while hot and add brandy. Add brown sugar, ginger, and cinnamon. Let set overnight.

TO SERVE: Core remaining 6 apples, stud with cloves and bake until tender. Place in punch bowl and add brandy mixture. Add water. Serve with a dash of nutmeg.

MULLED WINE I

6	egg yolks	$^{1}/_{2}$ cup	sugar
dash	ground cinnamon	dash	ground cloves
4 cups	white wine, heated to boiling		

Beat egg yolks. Beat in sugar and spices. Slowly pour boiling wine into egg mixture, stirring constantly. The warm wine will cook the egg. Serve warm.

MULLED WINE II

$^{1}/_{4}$ cup	water	$^{1}/_{2}$ cup	sugar
1 stick	cinnamon	1 slice	lemon
6	whole cloves	dash	nutmeg
1 bottle	red wine	$^{1}/_{2}$ cup	brandy

Simmer water and sugar, until sugar dissolves. Add cinnamon, lemon studded with the cloves, and fresh grated nutmeg. Add wine and heat, but do not boil. Add brandy and serve.

John Askin to Charles Patterson at Montreal, June 17, 1778:

Your friends in this quarter have thought themselves very happy to have a dance once a week & entertain their Company with a dish of Tea & humble Grogg during the last winter, whilst you at London could have all your wants & wishes Supplied, as well as your wanton wishes. [1]

John Askin to James Sterling at Detroit, May 8, 1778:

I received the Wine & Tea by Mr Bennett which came very Seasonably [3]

Silver punch bowl given to Major De Peyster when he left Michilimackinac.

RED WINE PUNCH I

3 cups	red wine	2 cups	fresh tea
1/2 cup	rum	3/4 cup	sugar
juice of 2 lemons			

Mix together wine, tea, rum, and sugar. Heat to boiling. Add lemon juice. Serve hot or cold.

RED WINE PUNCH II

2 qts	strawberries, crushed		
1 cup	sugar	1/2 cup	lemon juice
1/2 gal	red wine		

Combine ingredients; chill 1 hour. Serve.

WASSAIL BOWL

1 qt	apple cider	1/2 tsp	nutmeg
1 stick	cinnamon	1 tsp	ground ginger
2 cups	sugar	2 bottles	sherry
		1 lg bottle	ale
		1 qt	cranberry juice
		1	apple or orange studded with cloves.

Bring cider and spices to a boil and simmer 10 minutes. Add sugar, sherry, ale. Stir over low heat until sugar dissolves. Pour into a punch bowl, adding cranberry juice. Float fruit in the bowl.

SYLLABUB

1 cup	Madeira wine	*or*	½ cup	brandy or cider
1 cup	white wine		1 cup	sugar
4 cups	heavy cream			nutmeg

Combine sugar and wines in a mixing bowl. Gradually beat in cream until it forms soft peaks. Spoon into glasses and top with fresh grated nutmeg.

An old recipe from Amelia Simmons suggests you "milk your cow into the liquor." [4]

CIDER POSSET

2 cups	apple cider	4 cups	heavy cream
10 egg	yolks	4 egg	whites
1 cup	Madeira wine		grated nutmeg

Mix cream and cider. Beat egg yolks until smooth and add to cider. Beat egg whites in a separate bowl. Fold into cider mixture. Add Madeira. Simmer over low heat until mixture thickens. Serve warm or cold. Top with nutmeg.

RUM

HOT BUTTERED RUM

1 lump	sugar	1 cup	hot cider
1 jigger	rum	1 tsp	butter
¼ tsp	cinnamon		fresh grated nutmeg

Mix sugar and 2 T of the hot cider in a mug. Add butter, rum and cinnamon. Stir and fill with hot cider. Sprinkle with grated nutmeg.

*Welcome **Logbook Wednesday, 3d November, 1779:***

About 11 A.M. two Negroes of a Party that had been driven over to the Isld with a Raft of Timber, came on Board, to whom I gave provisions and Rum. [5]

John Porteous, Michilimackinac, 1767:

Here are three or four kinds of the Spruce pine, one of which is the best for making beer of any on ye Continent, as far as I can learn, & can only be equalled in Newfoundland, Anor of them is reputed & experienced by the French here an infallible cure for the most inveterate scurvey, & indeed all spruce is reckoned a good antescurbutic, either in decoction or beer. Within these 2 years the beer is become the most usual table drink in all our provinces, being first brot [brought] into practice in the army by Genl Amherst in some of his Campaigns. [6]

Switchel was a mid-afternoon drink, commonly served to men working in fields doing heavy labor. When they cut hay or meadow grass, chopped wood, or split a pile of shingles, they may have welcomed this drink.

SPRUCE BEER [7]
From Fort Ticonderoga

"Take **7 pounds of good Spruce** and boil it well till the bark peels off, then take the Spruce out & put **three Gallons of Molasses** to the Liquor & boil it again, scum it well as it boils, then take it out the Kettle & put it into a cooler Welcome; boil the remainder of the Water sufficient for a Barrel of thirty Gallons, if the Kettle is not large enough to boil it together; When milkwarm in the Cooler put a **Pint of Yest** into it and mix well. Then put in the Barrel and let it work for two or three days, keep filling it up as it works out. When done working, bung it up with a Tent Peg in the Barrel to give it vent every now and then. It may be used in two or three days after. If wanted to be bottled it should stand a fortnight in the cask. It will keep a great while."

SHRUB
Sweetened Berry Juice

Place **raspberries** in a crock, cover with **vinegar, brandy, or rum,** and let stand overnight. Strain through a cloth and measure the juice. For each quart of juice, add **3 cups of sugar**. Boil 30 minutes and pour into a bottle.

To serve, dilute with 2 parts water or white wine and pour over ice.

SWITCHEL

2 quarts	hot water	**1 cup**	sugar
1/2 cup	molasses	**1/2 cup**	vinegar
1/2 tsp	crushed ginger		

Mix together and let cool. Used much like the Gatorade products are used by sports enthusiasts today.

COFFEE

Many a reenactor has tried to figure out how to make a morning pot of coffee without using their automatic coffee maker. Modern cooks have been spoiled with the ease of premeasured, preground filter packs and automatically controlled coffee makers or espresso machines. We aren't used to swallowing the coffee grounds with our beverage and many folks forego their morning cup, rather than try to strain the grounds out.

To brew coffee 18th-century style, try this method: Rinse a coffee pot or covered kettle with hot water. Place fresh grounds ($1/2$ cup for 6 cups of water) on the bottom. Break an egg over the grounds, laying the crushed shell on top of them. Add a pinch of salt and $1/2$ cup of cold water. Stir until blended. Add 6 cups of boiling water to the pot, cover, and heat until it comes to a full boil. Simmer 3-4 minutes and then allow to steep. The egg and shell will coagulate with the grounds in the bottom of the pot and the coffee should be good and clear.

Lotbinière, 1749:

The women are no more laborious than the men. They put on lady-like airs and to keep up appearances they spend time, every day going from house to house for a cup of coffee or chocolate.[8]

CHOCOLATE

The chocolate of the 18th century was a very bitter, dark chocolate. It is most similar to bars of baking chocolate, not the sweetened milk chocolate we are used to today. It was prepared in a special "chocolate pot." The chocolate was melted and sugar was added. Then it was stirred into scalded milk and served as a hot drink. Nutmeg was often used to season it.

TEA

Tea was imported and some of the records and artifacts show it to be common in the upper class. Elizabeth Scott, in her

John Askin to Sampson Fleming at Detroit, April 28, 1778:

Mrs Askin has still some Tea & loaf Sugar & once a Day for herself will be able to hold out, the rest of us have Chocolate for Breakfast & Barly Substituted in the room for Coffe for the afternoon Spirits & Spruce we have & can & must do without wine for the Present.[9]

Teas mentioned on Askin's lists:

best green tea

common green tea

fine Hyson Tea

Bohea tea

His household inventory and trade lists included:

large red Tea Potts

small Plated Tea Potts

black Tea pott, sugar dish & milk pott

large Japaned Tea Board

small Tea Spoons & Tongs

China

dissertation "Such Diet as Befitted His Station as Clerk," wrote:

> Using only the written records, one might gain the impression that tea-drinking was an activity only of the wealthy at Michilimackinac. However tea wares of varying qualities were found in the refuse of all the households examined here. Perhaps tea-drinking as a formal social event was an upper class British activity at Michilimackinac, but tea-drinking itself was common.[10]

The art of brewing and serving tea was quite formal. A tea table would be set with a teapot, slop bowl, container for milk or cream, tea canister, sugar bowl and tongs, teaspoons, and cups and saucers. The teapot was usually placed in the center of the table. A hot water kettle would sit on a nearby table or stand, full of boiling water. Guests would exchange gossip and news while waiting for the tea to brew. Sometimes the tea was poured through a strainer, into the cups, to remove the loose tea leaves. Before a teacup was refilled, the remaining tea or grounds were emptied into a slop bowl. The cup would be rinsed out and refilled from the fresh-brewed china pot.[11]

HERBAL TEAS

It is likely that, at least among the Native American population, herbal teas were used at Mackinac. They were free, as all one had to do was go for a walk along the beach or in the nearby woods to gather the leaves, roots, and flowers. These were dried and saved for later use or used fresh. Many had medicinal values, to cure headaches or stomachaches, or at least as a tonic for spring fever.

The following herbal teas are listed as commonly used among Native American populations.[13] These all grow in the area and might have been used here.

Acorn shells were roasted and steeped;

Bearberry (kinnikinnick or upland cranberry) leaves were brewed to soothe a stomach;

Bergamot (bee balm or oswego tea) leaves were a tea for sore throats and settling stomachs;

Blackberry leaves made a tea to relieve diarrhea;

Borage leaves and flowers made a tonic to cure a cough;

Chicory leaves and blossoms were steeped to relieve mucus congestion;

Clover leaves and blossoms were used as a diuretic to cure urinary tract infections;

Comfrey leaves and roots provided internal and external healing;

Goldenrod leaves and flowers reduced phlegm;

Mint leaves made a beverage to soothe the stomach;

Pennyroyal (squawbalm, squawmint) leaves were used to relieve headaches and cramps;

Rose hips, high in vitamin C, prevented scurvy;

Sassafras leaves, roots, and bark reduced fevers and acted as a spring tonic;

Sumac berries relieved kidney infections;

Wild chamomile leaves and blossoms were used internally to relieve upset stomach, externally for earaches;

Witch Hazel leaves were dried and used for burns and insect bites.

John Porteous, 1767:

In many places there is also several Sorts of pine, & other barren Woods of most kinds in this neighborhood, & the woods are all overgrown with gooseberries, Currens, Strawberries, raspberries, &c.&c.&c. in amazing quantities; besides, numberless Simple medicinal Shrubs are found here in great plenty, a detail of which I shall forbear to mention.[12]

Redware teapot

MISCELLANEOUS RECIPES

THIS CHAPTER IS A COLLECTION of various foodstuffs, including preserves, pickled foods, condiments, and maple sugar. Many of these recipes are the preserved forms of the crops harvested during the summer and fall. Some of these items would have been found stored in root cellars or attics, or hanging from the rafters.

Preserving fruits, jellies, butters and jams in the 18th century tested a cook's ability to prevent spoilage and mold from forming. This was before the days of canning jars, tin cans, Tupperware, and plastic wrap. Preserves were placed in crocks or glasses and often sealed with a paper circle that had been dipped in brandy or rum. Another method was to top a bottle with a cork and then apply pitch or wax to make a seal. Some glasses were sealed with layers of thin paper tied tightly, and then coated with a thin layer of egg white. Large pickle crocks were sealed with animal bladders. These were stored in a salt brine to keep them soft. They were tied onto a jar and had to be kept moist by brushing daily with a salt water solution.

Fresh fruits, like apples and pears, and vegetables, like carrots and beets, could be stored in root cellars. They were placed in a barrel with oats, sand, leaves, or straw to surround each one. The packing material would help retain moisture and prevent the food from shriveling up. Cabbages were wrapped in their outer leaves and separated with layers of damp moss. These foods had to be kept cold, but not frozen. The moderately cool temperature would help retard ripening and slow the start of fermentation. They had to be checked over and any rotten fruit

removed because "one rotten apple will spoil the whole bunch." Windfall apples were not saved this way as they were usually bruised. These would be made into apple butter or sauce, or dried.

Smaller fruits like strawberries and huckleberries could simply be dried. They were washed and hulled and laid on a clean cloth in the sun. It takes 2-3 sunny days to complete the drying. The berries need to be brought in at night, before the dew dampens them. At Michilimackinac, we cover them with a cheesecloth to disguise them from the sea gulls who are looking for a sweet treat! The berries can be stored in a bottle or crock and used like raisins. Native Americans preserved wild berries and fruits by making a sun-dried fruit cake. They boiled blueberries, currants, cherries, raspberries, plums or other small fruit for half an hour. They then laid it on pans, bark or leaves, in the sun to dry. When partially dry, it was cut in blocks, turned over, and sprinkled with maple sugar. It was stored for later.

Some root crops were simply stored underground in a trench. A hole was dug below the frost line. The food was laid in the bottom and covered loosely with straw. A board might be placed over the trench to provide easier access. With Mackinac's "lake effect" snowfall this food would have been difficult to recover in the middle of winter!

Very ripe or windfall fruit would be made into "fruit leathers." They were cooked till soft, with very little water. They were then mashed and laid on plates, leaves, or cloths in the sun. Sometimes sugar was added. When dried, the leather could be cut into chunks or rolled up and stored in bags.

Another method to save small fruits like cherries was to preserve them in brandy. They were layered with sugar, in a crock, and then brandy was poured over. The tops could be sealed with an oiled or alcohol-soaked paper, a salt-brined animal bladder, a cork, or a wooden cover that was sealed with wax or pitch.

Some fruits were made into jams or preserves. These jars were often topped with paper that was brushed with egg white. This was sticky and would also shrink up the paper and make it tight as a drum. Some of the crocks had a lip around the rim. A wood or pottery lid which fit tightly could be placed on the crock and then sealed with melted wax.

One specific reference we have about how apples might have been used is a letter written by Archange Meredith Askin. A daughter of John Askin, she had married a soldier and followed him to Woolwich, England. From there, she often wrote her mother. On September 2, 1794, she wrote home asking for a favorite recipe. Unfortunately, we do not have the response to this letter.

APPLE JELLY

| 4 cups | apple juice *(instructions below)* |
| 3 cups | sugar |

TO PREPARE JUICE:
Select **3 lbs ripe to fully ripe apples**. Sort, wash, and remove the stem and blossom ends; do not pare or core. Cut apples into small pieces. Add **3 cups water**, cover, and bring to a boil on high heat. Reduce heat and simmer 25 minutes, until apples are soft. Extract the juice by straining through a jelly bag.

TO MAKE JELLY:
Measure juice into a large saucepan. Add sugar and stir well. Boil over high heat to 220° or until jelly sheets from a spoon. Remove from heat. Skim foam. MODERN: Pour into hot, sterilized jars, leaving $1/4$ inch head space. Process in a boiling water bath for 5 minutes. TRADITIONAL: Store in a crock in a cool place. Seal jars by laying a greased paper on the surface, or by tying an animal bladder or stomach over the crock, much like modern plastic wrap.

Archange Meredith Askin from Woolwich, England to her mother, September 2, 1794:

For a long time I have wanted to ask you how to make apple jelly. You will doubtless be surprised at such a request, but I assure you no one here knows how and never even has heard of it. As my dear husband has what the English call a **sweet tooth,** *I want to cram that tooth for him with something good. He often speaks of that delicious apple jelly, and every time he mentions it, I am sorry that I do not know how to make it. Please, dear Mother, teach me that secret by the first chance you have after receiving this, that is, if the French allow this letter to reach you.*[1]

APPLE BUTTER

| 6 lbs | apples | 5 lbs | brown sugar |
| 1 T | ground cinnamon | 1 T | vinegar |

Wash apples, cut into quarters, and cook in **4 cups water** until tender. Pass through a sieve to remove the skin and the seeds. Measure out 1 gallon of stewed apples. Add sugar, cinnamon, and vinegar. Boil down to the thickness of marmalade. Pour into a crock and refrigerate. A modern cook can place in canning jars and process 10 minutes per pint.

RED CURRANT JELLY

| 4 lbs | red currants | 3 | whole cloves |
| | sugar | | |

Put currants and cloves in a saucepan and simmer until soft and mushy. Strain through a jelly bag. Do not squeeze the fruit or your jelly will be cloudy. Let set several hours or overnight.

Measure juice and add an equal amount of sugar. Stir over low heat until sugar is dissolved. Bring to a boil for 10 minutes, until jelly begins to set. Pour into jars, seal, and process in a boiling water bath.

PICKLED FOODS

Pickled foods were made from vinegars. This was generally apple cider vinegar. Sometimes a special herbal vinegar was made, as in the following recipe.

TARRAGON VINEGAR

Wash **fresh tarragon leaves** and fill a bottle half full. Fill bottle with **cider vinegar**, cover, and set aside for a week. Replace tarragon leaves with fresh leaves, cover, and use as needed.

MAPLE WATER VINEGAR

Maple water vinegar was made in Upper Canada. When the **sap** became poor for sugar, it was boiled down to about $1/3$ of its volume and cooled. **Yeast** was then added. It was placed in a barrel, in a warm place, and allowed to ferment. In a few weeks it was ready to use to pickle meats and vegetables.

CROCK BRINED DILL PICKLES

10 lbs	dill size cucumbers
1$1/2$ cups	pickling salt
2 cups	cider vinegar
2 heads	garlic, separated into cloves
1 bunch	fresh dill weed and flower heads

2 gal   water

Wash and scald out a pickle crock. Make sure you have a lid or at least a cloth cover that fits. Wash and drain cukes. Remove any spoiled, soft, or bruised fruit and use elsewhere. If cukes are very large they can be sliced into chunks or spears. Wash dill by submerging underwater. Any little bugs will float to the surface and can be removed. Peel garlic cloves. Layer cukes, dill, and garlic until crock is full. Pack as tightly as possible.

Mix vinegar, salt, and water. Heat until the salt is all dissolved. Pour over the cukes when cooled to lukewarm. Weight cukes under the brine with a plate. A clean, heavy rock on the plate will keep the cukes submerged. In a modern kitchen, fill a plastic ziplock bag with extra brine and lay it on the surface. This will weight it down and if the bag leaks, it's just more brine.

Store the container at about 70°, and let cukes ferment. Remove scum daily, as it develops. (It's not spoiling.) Our staff start eating them in a matter of a few hours, but they'll reach their best flavor in 2-3 weeks.

MUSTARD

2 T	mustard seed	2 cloves	minced garlic
6 T	olive oil		
6 T	vinegar (Try the tarragon vinegar on page 190.)		

Pound mustard seed with a mortar and pestle until powdery (or substitute dry mustard). Add garlic, stir in vinegar, blending well. Gradually blend in olive oil. Mix well. Bottle for use with beef or lamb.

HORSERADISH SAUCE

This sauce is very good with beef—or to cover up the taste of meat that has been kept a little too long!

3 T	fresh grated horseradish root		
½ cup	whipping cream		
1 tsp	vinegar	1 tsp	lemon juice
½ tsp	sugar	¼ tsp	dry mustard
	salt		

Mix all ingredients except cream in a bowl. Whip cream and fold into other ingredients. Chill at least 3 hours and use as needed. (Use fresh, as cream will sour in a few days.)

SUGAR

When today's visitors walk the streets of Mackinaw City or Mackinac Island, one of the first things they notice is the smell of sugar coming from the many fudge, caramel corn, and ice cream shops. A first impression is that the local economy is based on tourists buying these sugar products. It is not until we look at historical documents and diaries that we begin to gather the full importance of sugar and candy to the Mackinac region.

In earlier years sugar didn't come in a bag from a grocery

store. It was a valuable commodity that required much effort to obtain. British sailing ships made trading trips to Barbados and various West Indian tropical islands where sugar cane was grown and processed on sugar plantations. White, processed sugar was very expensive and used sparingly to sweeten tea or to make cakes. It came in a cone shape, wrapped in blue paper, and had to be crushed and pounded with a mortar and pestle or cut from the cone with a tool called a sugar nipper. These cones of sugar were shipped from the Indies back to England and then traded throughout the world at major sea ports.

The expense of white sugar would have kept it out of the hands of most soldiers, traders, and early pioneers living in the wilderness. However, as we examine the literature we find that maple sugar was made and used in place of white, refined cane sugar. The Indians and the French produced huge quantities of maple sugar during the spring sap run. The residents moved out into the woods and set up sugar camps. There they collected and boiled down the sap into the more usable sugar. This could be stored and used later or traded for other goods.

The following poem was written by Arent Schuyler De Peyster, who commanded the British garrison at Michilimackinac from 1774 to 1779.

THE MAPLE SUGAR MAKERS
Tune: Jolly Beggars

I'll sling my papoo's cradle, said Kitchenegoe's Meg,
With kettle, bowl, and ladle, and scoutawaba [rum] keg.
A sug'ring I will go, will go, will go,

A sug'ring I will go.

Nasib and Charlotte Farlie, of whom the lads are fond,
Shall drag their father early out to the twelve mile pond.
 A sug'ring I will go, & c.

Come, Nebenaquoidoquoi, and join the jovial crew,
Sheeshib and Matchinoquoi shall tap a tree with you,
 A sug'ring I will go, & c.

Bright Kesis [sun], deign to aid us, and make the sap to run,
Eninga, [De Peyster's wife Rebecca] who arrayed us, at least
should have a tun,
 A sug'ring I will go, & c.

In kettles we will boil it, on fires between the rocks,
And lest the snow should spoil it, there tramp it in mococks
[birch bark containers],
 A sug'ring I will go, & c.

Of all our occupations, sweet sug'ring is the best,
Then girls and their relations can give their lovers rest,
 A sug'ring I will go, & c.

But when the season's over, it will not
    be amiss,
That I should give my lover a sissobaquet
    [sugar or sweet] kiss,
 A sug'ring we will go, & c. [2]

Indian maple sugar camp, drawn by Seth Eastman.

Maple Snow

Boil **maple syrup** until it reaches 230-250° on a candy thermometer. Drizzle over a bowl of clean, hardpacked snow. The syrup will harden instantly into a chewy taffy. Delicious!

Maple Sugar Fudge

2 cups	maple sugar	$^1/_2$ pint	cream

Combine in a pan and boil to 240° (soft ball stage). Remove from heat and cool to lukewarm. Beat until the texture is dull and the fudge thickens. Pour into a small buttered cake pan and let set. Eat and enjoy!

Another Maple Fudge

3 cups	brown sugar	$^1/_3$ cup	maple syrup
$1^1/_3$ cups	milk	2 T	butter
pinch	salt	$^1/_2$ tsp	vanilla
$^1/_2$ cup	nutmeats		

Combine ingredients, except vanilla and nuts. Stir over low heat until dissolved. Boil to the soft ball stage, without stirring. Cool and beat until thick and creamy. Add vanilla and nuts. Pour into a greased pan and cut before it hardens.

Maple Pralines

2 cups	maple syrup	$^1/_2$ cup	pecans or walnuts

Cook syrup until it makes a soft ball in cold water. Let stand one minute and then pour into a lightly buttered pie tin. Sprinkle with broken nutmeats. Let harden.

Looking for real maple sugar?

We get ours from Ralph Snow, Snow Sugar Shack, 3188 Plains Road, Mason, Michigan 48854 517-676-2442.

What would a Mackinac cookbook be without a recipe for fudge? Try this simple maple candy. Make sure you use real maple syrup!

MAPLE POPCORN

We can't prove this is historically accurate to the 18th century at Michilimackinac, but what is Mackinac without a recipe for its famous caramel corn?

2 cups	sugar	¹/₂ cup	maple syrup
1¹/₂ cups	water	1 tsp	vinegar
¹/₂ tsp	salt	1 tsp	maple flavoring
5 qts	popped corn		

Butter the sides of a large pan. Combine sugar, syrup, water, vinegar and salt. Cook to the hardball stage. Stir in maple flavoring. Slowly pour mixture over popped corn, mixing gently. Butter your hands and shape popcorn into small balls.

RENDERED FATS

Alexander Henry, 1762:

At the same time that I paid the price which I have mentioned for maize I paid at the rate of a dollar per pound for the tallow, or prepared fat to mix with it. The meat itself was at the same price. The Jesuit missionary killed an ox which he sold by the quarter, taking the weight of the meat in beaver skin.[3]

Fat was rendered or melted and stored away to use like we use vegetable shortening today. The **fat** was collected and placed in a large kettle. A couple inches of **water** was placed in the bottom to prevent smoking and burning. Today we add **a tablespoon of baking soda**, but they probably used **wood ash**. This makes the impurities foam and rise to the surface where they can be skimmed off. When the fat is melted, skim the surface and allow it to sit. As it hardens, the fat will float above the water and impurities will sink to the bottom. Remove the fat, pouring off the water. Reprocess, if it smells bad, is old fat, or if it still has impurities. The fat was stored in a cool place, in a crock with a lid. If it began to smell bad, it could be sweetened by remelting with additional soda.

This rendered fat or lard was used for cooking. This was the grease used to coat pans, to make a pie dough, or to use in other baking. It was also the source of soap. During the Fall Harvest Festivals at Michilimackinac we have been making our own soap. We do this outdoors, over an open fire. Many visitors have asked for the recipe, so it is included here. Many thanks go to those who have helped stir and offered advice, as this was a new project and we had no experience at it. Now, we have had many successful batches and many a visitor has had a chance to try a bar of fresh lye soap!

SOAP

3 cups	rendered fat (beef suet or lard)
1/4 cup	lye crystals (Red Devil brand)
1 cup	water

Render fat, strain, cool, and measure. Reheat till it is melted. In a second kettle (a glass or enamel pan which you will not use again for food), mix lye and water. Stir the lye flakes into cold water, and stir with a wooden spoon until dissolved.

Carefully pour melted fat into the lye, being careful not to splash on your skin. Stir until thick and creamy, like fudge. This may take up to an hour.

Pour into a mold. We use a cloth-lined bowl but you may want to line an old shoe box with wax paper and use that. Age your soap at least two weeks. It will harden as it sets.

VARIATIONS:

The soaps may be scented with essential oils. These oils are available at pharmacies, health food stores, and some herb shops. A few drops of oil are added just before pouring into the mold. Proper 18th-century scents would include lavender, rose, and strawberry.

Chamomile, cherry, apple, rose, or lavender blossoms may be placed in the mold and the soap poured over them. The fat in the soap will pick up the scent and retain it.

A pine soap may be made by boiling 2 cups pine needles with 1 cup water to form a strong tea. The water is poured off and used with lye to make the soap. We make a special pumice soap for our blacksmith. Just before pouring the soap into the mold, add 1 cup of fine, sifted sand. This will add grit and help remove ground-in dirt.

Soap making requires a strong lye solution. The easiest and most practical solution for most people, including us, has been to purchase lye crystals (Red Devil toilet bowl cleaner). Homemade lye takes time, a supply of hardwood ashes, and luck to produce. As a safety factor, we don't want a barrel of raw lye sitting around a state park site. It would be too easy for a curious visitor or dog to be burned.

Whenever working with lye, be very careful not to splash it on your skin or clothing. Also, wear safety glasses. If some should get on you, wash it off immediately, with lots of clear water.

Herbal Remedies

Horehound Drops

These "cough drops" were used for sore throats and to relieve lung congestion.

1 cup   horehound leaves and stems
1½ cups hot water   2⅓ cups brown sugar

Crush herbs and cover with hot water. Steep like a tea for 30 minutes. Strain and pour tea into brown sugar. Bring to a boil until it reaches the hard crack stage (300°). Pour into a buttered pan, let cool and break into chunks. (Made like hard crack Christmas candy.)

Onion Poultice

An onion poultice was used when a patient suffered from pneumonia or had difficulty breathing. Start by chopping **6-10 onions**. Fry them over a hot fire. Add equal parts of of **rye meal** and **vinegar** to form a stiff paste. Stir thoroughly and simmer 10 minutes. Put in a cloth bag and apply to the patient's chest as hot as he or she can stand. Change every 10 minutes, reheating onions and reapplying until the patient breathes easier.

EPILOGUE

AS YOU VISIT THE STRAITS AREA today, take time to reflect on how much we share in common with those who lived here in the past. It is sometimes uncanny to look at how similar life in Mackinac is today to how it was 250 years ago. It is still the "Crossroads of the North," as travelers throughout the Midwest sail through the straits or drive over the Mackinac Bridge. The island continues to draw visitors like a magnet as they come to spend their vacations.

During the winter the streets are quiet and the locals spend a lot of time hunting and ice fishing. The sound of gas-driven wood splitters has replaced the sound of axes, but there is still the smell of woodsmoke in the air. Ice fishermen chop holes in the ice so they can catch perch, walleye, and pike. People like to get out in the woods, although they use snowmobiles and 4-wheelers more often than snowshoes. Dogsleds still fill the streets of Mackinac in the winter as the "Mushers" gather to race. Every April morning the locals wake up, look out their windows, and check to see if the ice is breaking up.

As spring approaches, the local businessmen begin to write orders, take inventory, and get their stores ready to open. (Even the local McDonald's closes for the winter!) During the spring there are still many families who have a home business or hobby, producing a few quarts of maple syrup from the trees in their yards. The ferry companies begin to service their boats and get them ready to go back into the water. Locals meet at the coffee shop and talk about what they expect for the next summer's tourist season.

As summer begins, the shops open for business. Wholesalers ship goods in from the cities. Vacationers come with their savings, earned elsewhere during the winter, and purchase lots of items in the local gift shops. They use money, instead of furs, but this is still where that exchange takes place. You can still hear the sound of bartering at the many craft shows and art fairs. Summer residents open up their cottages and begin to visit with their neighbors, catching up on the news of the last few months.

Ferry boats begin their regular service to Mackinac Island. They carry more people and go out in rougher weather than the canoes of the past, but it is still the primary way to reach the island. The freighters pass by, carrying iron ore and grain. They are propelled by engines rather than oars, but they remind us of the large *canots de maître* which freighted the furs, corn, and trade goods. The town sometimes fills up with stranded motorists as the bridge is occasionally closed to traffic during high winds. It reminds us that those canoe men sometimes had to wait for calmer days before crossing the straits.

On Sunday mornings, you can still hear the church bells of Ste. Anne's on Mackinac Island. The parish continues today. In 1996, it celebrated its Tri-centennial, 300 years of life. The parish survived the move

to the island and went through several remodeling changes, but is still an active and vital part of the community.

The Native Americans are still an important part of the local community and economy. In the past they supplied corn to feed the troops. Later they fished the straits and lumbered the forests. Fishing is still a part of their life today. When stopping at Bell's Fishery to pick up fish for dinner, you will find them unloading their boats with fresh whitefish. Native fishermen, using nets, go out into the lakes and bring fish back daily. A lot of fish is consumed locally, but they also ship it out to other markets. Modern shipping means it will be shipped frozen rather than salted, but there is still a big call for the famous smoked whitefish.

Corn and maple sugar were important parts of the local economy in times past, and they continue to be so today. Visitors purchase pounds of fudge and boxes of caramel corn as they roam the shops and streets of Mackinac.

Rum and alcohol were an important part of the fur trade and there were many stories about the wild parties and excessive drinking during the summers of the 18th century. Perhaps the parties are a little quieter, but there are many local bars which have very successful summer businesses.

The French and British military used to be the governing force of the territory in days past. Today, the Governor has a summer home, located next to Fort Mackinac on the island. He hosts many conferences, and governors and governmental employees from around the country gather there. Many major unions and organizations host their summer conventions on the island, at Grand Hotel and other area resorts. Hillary Rodham Clinton came to the island in the summer of 1995 and George Bush walked the Mackinac Bridge during his 1994 campaign for the presidency. Mackinac is still "the place" to resort to.

As fall approaches, things begin to quiet down again. Summer residents begin to close up their cottages and prepare them for the winter storms. The stores hold sales to reduce their merchandise, because the market will decrease when the tourists leave. The college students who hold summer jobs in the area prepare to go back to school. There was no school at Fort Michilimackinac and residents sent their children to Detroit and Montreal to be educated. Today they send them to Michigan State University, Central Michigan University, the University of Michigan, and many other universities. The ferry boats come out of the water and are set up on blocks. The restaurants reduce their hours and some close up for the winter. Some of the shop owners prepare to leave and pursue a second career or job for the winter months.

The locals begin to clean their guns and get ready for hunting season. Many hunt ducks and geese as the birds migrate south. Others trap beaver for furs. Hunters take their dogs out to chase rabbits and grouse. The woods resound with gunfire as hunters "bag their buck." Deer hunters have several seasons—rifle, bow, and black powder. The fishermen begin to get their ice shanties ready. Island residents stock up on supplies before the ferry boats stop running.

As you visit Mackinaw City, take the time to walk around and see how the past influenced the present. Notice the street names—Etherington, Jamet, Louvigny, Ducharme, Marest. These are all names of fort people of the past. Reflect on the geography of the lakes and land and how it has influenced the lives of people who passed through here. Enjoy the summer climate and think about the winter storms to come. Look at the economy and recognize how important the fish, corn, and sugar are to it. Take time to go to some of the local restaurants and sample the whitefish dinners. Cross over the bridge and appreciate its convenience. Sail the waters and imagine being a voyageur of long ago. Reflect on the people who came before. And remember, Mackinac is truly a place of history.

NOTES

CHAPTER 1 - FOOD ON THE FRONTIER
1. Thwaites, Reuben Gold, *Collections of the State Historical Society of Wisconsin*, Vol. 17, pp. 359-60.

CHAPTER 3 - SOUPS
1. Thwaites, Reuben Gold, *The Jesuit Relations*, Vol. LXVI, p. 280.
2. Armour, David & Keith Widder, *At the Crossroads*, p. 218.
3. Quaife, Milo, editor, *John Askin Papers*, Vol. I, p. 54.
4. *Michigan Pioneer and Historical Collections (MPHC)*, Vol. 10, p. 326.
5. Kimball, Marie, *Thomas Jefferson's Cookbook*, p. 47.
6. Armour, David, *Attack at Michilimackinac*, p. 34.
7. Mason, Philip, *Indian Thoroughfares Provided Routes for State's Modern Highways,* p. 3-4.
8. *MPHC*, Vol. 14, p. 644.
9. Kalm, Peter, *Peter Kalm's Travels*, p. 92.
10. *Askin Papers*, Vol. I, p. 51.
11. *Askin Papers*, Vol. I, p. 54.
12. *Askin Papers*, Vol. I, p. 55.
13. Glasse, Hannah, *The Art of Cookery*, p. 184.
14. Gardiner, Anne, *Mrs. Gardiner's Family Recipes*, p. 7.
15. *Askin Papers*, Vol. I, p. 57.
16. *Askin Papers*, Vol. I, p. 52.
17. Thwaites, *The Jesuit Relations*, Vol. XV, p. 163.

CHAPTER 4 - MAIN DISHES
1. Garmey, Jane, *Great British Cooking*, p. 64.
2. Armour & Widder, *Crossroads*, p. 80.
3. *Askin Papers*, Vol. I, p. 78.
4. Armour, *Attack*, pp. 82-83.
5. Armour, *Attack*, p. 86.
6. *Askin Papers*, Vol. I, p. 137.
7. *MPHC*, Vol. 9, p. 540.
8. Gérin-Lajoie, Marie, *Fort Michilimackinac in 1749: Lotbinière's Plan and Description*, p. 9.
9. *Welcome*, Logbook.
10. *Askin Papers*, Vol. I, p. 54-56.
11. *Askin Papers*, Vol. I, p. 54-58.
12. *MPHC*, Vol. 11, p. 332.
13. *Askin Papers*, Vol. I, p. 54.
14. Scott, Elizabeth, *Such Diet as Befitted His Station as Clerk*, p. 147.
15. Armour, *At the Crossroads*, pp. 210, 223.
16. Scott, pp.147-148.
17. *Askin Papers*, Vol. I, p. 54.
18. Armour, *Attack*, p. 33.
19. *Askin Papers*, Vol. I, p. 54.
20. Porteous, John, *Journal From Schenectady to Michilimackinac & the Channels 1765 & 1766*, pp. 96-97.
21. *Old French Town Cookery*.
22. *Askin Papers*, Vol. I, p. 54.

CHAPTER 5 - FISH
1. Armour, *Attack*, pp. 34, 38.
2. Thwaites, Reuben Gold, editor, *New Voyages to North America, by the Baron De Lahontan*, Vol. I, p. 147.
3. Crump, Nancy, *Hearthside Cooking*, p. 158.
4. *Wisconsin Historical Collections*, Vol. 7, p. 175.
5. *MPHC*, Vol. 9, p. 540.
6. Garmey, p. 3.
7. Dunton, Hope, *From the Hearth*, p. 33.
8. Gates, Charles M., editor, *Five Fur Traders of the Northwest*, p. 32.
9. Armour, *Attack*, pp. 33-34.
10. Kavasch, Barrie, *Native Harvests*, p. 102.
11. Gérin-Lajoie, p.9.

CHAPTER 6 - BREADS
1. *Askin Papers,* Vol. I, pp. 52-56.
2. Boily, Lise, & Jean-Francois Blanchett, *The Bread Ovens of Québec.*
3. Silitch, Clarissa, *Old Farmer's Almanac Colonial Cookbook,* p. 15.
4. Silitch, p. 19.
5. *Askin Papers,* Vol. I, pp. 70-72.
6. Leuke, Barbara K., *Feeding the Frontier Army, 1775-1865,* p. 30.
7. *Askin Papers,* Vol. I, p. 53.
8. *Askin Papers,* Vol. I, p. 75.
9. *Welcome,* Logbook.
10. *Askin Papers,* Vol. I, pp. 78-79.
11. *Askin Papers,* Vol. I, pp. 105-107.

CHAPTER 7 - VEGETABLES & FRUITS
1. Armour & Widder, *Crossroads,* pp. 209-222.
2. Sterling, James, *A Letterbook,* p. 61.
3. Ford, Richard, *Corn From the Straits of Mackinac,* p. 97.
4. Armour, *Attack,* p. 29.
5. Armour, *Attack,* p. 33.
6. Armour & Widder, *Crossroads,* pp. 209-236.
7. Parker, John, editor, *The Journals of Jonathan Carver and Related Documents, 1766-1770,* p. 74.
8. *Askin Papers,* Vol. I, p. 53.
9. Heldman, Donald P., *Excavations at Fort Michilimackinac, 1976: The Southeast and South Southeast Row Houses,* pp. 182-187.
10. *Askin Papers,* Vol. I, pp. 50-57.
11. Garmey, p. 114.
12. *Askin Papers,* Vol. I, pp. 54-56.
13. *Askin Papers,* Vol. I, p. 55.
14. *Askin Papers,* Vol. I, pp. 55-56.
15. Kalm, p. 95.
16. *Askin Papers,* Vol. I, pp. 51, 55.
17. Corbett, Lucy, *French Cooking in Old Detroit,* p. 114.
18. *Askin Papers,* Vol. I, pp. 51-54.
19. Kalm, p. 183.
20. *Askin Papers,* Vol. II, p. 576.

CHAPTER 8 - DESSERTS
1. Armour & Widder, *Crossroads,* pp. 209-236.
2. *Recipes from the Raleigh Tavern Bake Shoppe,* p. 19.
3. Donovan, Hatrak, Mills & Shull, *The Thirteen Colonies Cookbook,* p. 92.
4. *Askin Papers,* Vol. I, pp. 67-68.
5. Pastor-Williams, Sara, *The National Trust Book of Traditional Puddings,* p. 6.
6. Silitch, p. 51.
7. Kalm, pp. 173-174.

CHAPTER 9 - BEVERAGES
1. *Askin Papers,* Vol. I, p. 135.
2. Gates, p. 47.
3. *Askin Papers,* Vol. I, p. 80.
4. Simmons, Amelia, *The First American Cookbook,* p. 31.
5. *Welcome,* Logbook.
6. Bald, F. Clever, editor, *From Niagara to Mackinac in 1767.*
7. *The Bulletin of the Fort Ticonderoga Museum,* Vol. 6, No. 6, p. 180.
8. Gérin-Lajoie, p. 9.
9. *Askin Papers,* Vol. I, p. 79.
10. Scott, pp. 121-122.
11. Roth, Rodris, *Tea Drinking in 18th-Century America: Its Etiquette and Equipage.*
12. Bald, p. 14.
13. Kavasch, pp. 129-138.

CHAPTER 10 - MISCELLANEOUS RECIPES
1. *Askin Papers,* Vol. I, pp. 516-517.
2. De Peyster, Arent Schuyler, *Miscellanies, by an Officer,* pp. 90-92.
3. Armour, *Attack,* p. 34.

HISTORICAL BIBLIOGRAPHY

"I cannot live without books."
Letter from Thomas Jefferson
to John Adams, June 10, 1815.

Aller, Wilma. "Aboriginal Food Utilization of Vegetation by the Indians of the Great Lakes Region as Recorded in *The Jesuit Relations.*" *Wisconsin Archaeologist,* Vol. 35, Issue 3, pp. 59-73, 1952.

Armour, David A., Editor. *Attack at Michilimackinac: Alexander Henry's Travels and Adventures in Canada and the Indian Territories Between the Years 1760 and 1764.* Mackinac Island State Park Commission, 1971, originally published in 1809 by Alexander Henry.

_____. "David and Elizabeth," *Mackinac History,* Vol. II, No. 6. Mackinac Island, 1982.

_____. "Made in Mackinac," *Mackinac History,* Vol. I, No. 8. Mackinac Island, 1966.

_____. "Women at Michilimackinac," *Mackinac History,* Vol. 1, No. 10. Mackinac Island, 1967.

_____ & Keith R. Widder. *At the Crossroads, Michilimackinac During the American Revolution.* Mackinac Island, 1986.

Bald, F. Clever. *From Niagara to Mackinac in 1767.* Detroit, 1938.

Baron, Robert. *The Garden and Farm Books of Thomas Jefferson.* Fulcrum, Colorado, 1987.

Belote, Julianne. *The Compleat American Housewife.* Concord, CA, 1974.

Blake, Leonard and Hugh Cutler. *Cultivated Plants from Fort Michilimackinac, 1770-1780.* Missouri Botanical Garden, 1969.

Booth, Sally Smith. *Hung, Strung & Potted, A History of Eating Habits in Colonial America.* New York, 1971.

Brown, Henry, et al. *Cadillac and the Founding of Detroit.* Detroit, 1979.

Charlevoix, Pierre de. *Journal of a Voyage to North America,* March of America Facsimile Series No. 36. Ann Arbor, 1966.

Cleland, Charles. *The Prehistoric Animal Ecology and Ethnozoology of the Upper Great Lakes Region,* Anthropological Papers No. 29. Museum of Anthropology, University of Michigan, Ann Arbor, 1966.

Clifton, James, George Cornell and James McClurken. *The People of the Three Fires.* Grand Rapids, 1987.

Collections of the State Historical Society of Wisconsin, Vol. 17. Madison, WI, 1906.

Danzinger, Edmond Jefferson. *The Chippewas of Lake Superior.* Norman, OK, 1978.

Densmore, Frances. *Chippewa Customs.* St. Paul, MN, 1979.

DePeyster, Arent Schuyler. *Miscellanies by an Officer.* Dumfries, 1813.

Drummond, J.C. and Anne Wilbraham. *The Englishman's Food, A History of Five Centuries of English Diet.* London, 1969.

Dutton, Joan Parry. *Plants of Colonial Williamsburg.* Williamsburg, 1979.

Dunnigan, Brian Leigh. *The British Army at Mackinac 1812-1815.* Mackinac Island, 1980.

Earle, Alice. *Home Life in Colonial Days.* Middlevillage, New York, 1975.

Eberly, Carole, Editor. *Our Michigan Ethnic Tales and Recipes.* East Lansing, 1979.

Eccles, John. *The Canadian Frontier, 1534-1760.* New York, 1969.

Edmunds, R. David. *The Potawatomis, Keepers of the Fire.* Norman, Oklahoma, 1978.

Favretti, Rudy. *Early New England Gardens, 1620-1840.* Sturbridge, Massachusetts, 1961.

Fitting, James E. "Archaeological Excavations at the Marquette Mission Site, St. Ignace, Michigan, in 1972," *Michigan Archaeologist,* Vol. 22, Nos. 2-3.

Ford, Richard. "Corn From the Straits of Mackinac," *Michigan Archaeologist,* Vol. 20, No. 2, pp. 97-104, 1974.

Fort Ticonderoga. *The Bulletin of the Fort Ticonderoga Museum,* Vol. 6, No. 6, July, 1943

Gates, Charles M., Editor. *Five Fur Traders of the Northwest.* St. Paul, 1982.

Gérin-Lajoie, Marie. "Fort Michilimackinac in 1749: Lotbinière's Plan and Description," *Mackinac History,* Vol. II, No. 5. Mackinac Island, 1976.

Gilman, Carolyn. *Where Two Worlds Meet, The Great Lakes Fur Trade.* St. Paul, 1982.

Gringhus, Dirk. *Were Wolves and Will of the Wisps, French Tales of Mackinac Retold.* Mackinac Island, 1974.

Hardeman, Nicholas Perkins. *Shucks, Shocks and Hominy Blocks: Corn as a Way of Life in Pioneer America.* Baton Rouge, 1981.

Haughton, Claire Shaver. *Green Immigrants: The Plants that Transformed America.* New York, 1978.

Hayes, R. Vernon and Wilma Hays. *Foods the Indians Gave Us, How to Plant, Harvest and Cook the Natural Indian Way.* New York, 1973.

Hendrick, U.P. *A History of Horticulture in America to 1860.* Oxford, 1950.

Heldman, Donald P. *Archaeological Investigations at French Farm Lake in Northern Michigan 1981-82: A British Colonial Farm Site. Archaeological Completion Report Series,* No. 6. Mackinac Island, 1983.

_____. *Excavations at Fort Michilimackinac, 1976: The Southeast & South Southeast Row Houses. Archaeological Completion Report Series,* No. 1. Mackinac Island, 1977.

_____ and Roger T. Grange, Jr. *Excavations at Fort Michilimackinac; 1978-79, Rue de la Babillard, Archaeological Completion Report Series,* No. 3. Mackinac Island, 1981.

Heriot, George. *Travels Through the Canadas.* London, 1805.

Innis, Harold. *The Fur Trade in Canada.* Toronto, 1970.

Johnson, Ida Amanda. *The Michigan Fur Trade.* Grand Rapids, 1971.

Kalm, Peter. *Peter Kalm's Travels in North America, (The English Version of 1770).* Revised and edited by Adolph Benson. New York, 1966, 1987.

Kellogg, Louise P. *Early Narratives of the Northwest, 1634-1699.* New York, 1917.

Kinietz, Vernon. *The Indians of the Western Great Lakes, 1615-1760.* Ann Arbor, 1990, reprinted from 1940.

Kirk, Sylvia Van. *Many Tender Ties, Women in Fur Trade Society, 1670-1870.* Norman, Oklahoma, 1980.

Lahontan, Baron de. *New Voyages to North America.,* edited by Reuben Gold Thwaites, Vol. I and II. New York, reprint 1970.

Lehner, Ernst and Johanna Lehner. *Folklore & Odysseys of Food & Medicinal Plants.* New York, 1962.

Leighton, Ann. *American Gardens in the Eighteenth Century.* Amherst, 1976.

_____. *Early American Gardens, "For Meate or Medicine."* Amherst, 1970.

Long, John. *Voyages and Travels of an Indian Interpreter and Trader-1791.* Toronto, 1971.

MacCubbin, Robert and Peter Martin. *British and American Gardens in the Eighteenth Century.* Williamsburg, 1984.

Mangelsdorf, Paul. *Corn, Its Origin, Evolution and Improvement.* Cambridge, 1974.

Martin, Calvin. *Keepers of the Game, Indian-Animal Relationships and the Fur Trade.* Berkeley, 1978.

May, George. "The Askin Inventory," *Mackinac History,* Vol. I, No. 2. Mackinac Island, 1963.

_____. "The Mess at Mackinac or No More Sagamity for Me, Thank you," *Mackinac History,* Vol. I, No. 5. Mackinac Island, 1963.

_____. "Reconstruction of the Church of St. Anne de Michilimackinac," *Mackinac History,* Vol. I, No. 6. Mackinac Island, 1964.

May, George, Editor. *The Doctor's Secret Journal,* by Daniel Morison. Mackinac Island, 1960.

McClurken, James. *Gah-Baeh-Jhagwah-Buk, The Way It Happened.* Lansing, 1991.

Michigan Pioneer and Historical Society Collections, Vol. 9, 10, 11, 33, 34.

Niethammer, Carolyn. *American Indian Food and Lore.* New York, 1974.

Nute, Grace Lee. *The Voyageur.* St. Paul, 1987.

Parker, John, Editor. *Journals of Jonathan Carver and Related Documents 1766-1770.* St. Paul, 1976.

Peterson, Eugene. *France at Mackinac- A Pictorial Record of French Life and Culture 1715-1760.* Mackinac Island, 1968.

_____. *The Preservation of History at Mackinac.* Mackinac Island, 1972.

_____. *Mackinac and the Porcelain City.* Mackinac Island, 1985.

Peterson, Jacqueline. *The People in Between, Indian-White Marriage and the Genesis of a Métis Society and Culture in the Great Lakes Region, 1680-1830* (thesis). University of Illinois, 1981.

Porteous, John. "Journal from Schenectady to Michilimackinac and the Channels 1765 and 1766." Fred Hamil, Editor. *Ontario History,* Vol. 33 (1939).

Quaife, Milo, Editor. *John Askin Papers,* Vol. I & Vol II. Detroit, 1928.

Ranville, Judy and Nancy Campbell. *Memories of Mackinaw.* Mackinaw City, 1976.

Ray, Arthur and Donald Freeman. *Give Us Good Measure, An Economic Analysis of the Relations Between the Indians and the Hudson's Bay Company before 1763.* Toronto, 1978.

Root, Waverly and Richard de Rochemont. *Eating In America.* New York, 1976.

Roth, Rodris C. "Tea Drinking in 18th Century America, Its Etiquette & Equipage." *The United States National Museum,* Bulletin 225. Washington, D.C., 1961.

Rouse, John. *Cattle of North America.* Norman, Oklahoma, 1973.

Russell, Howard. *A Long Deep Furrow, Three Centuries of Farming in New England.* Hanover, 1982.

Russell, Doris. *Everyday Life in Colonial Canada.* London, 1973.

Sagard, Father Gabriel. *The Long Journey to the Country of the Hurons (1632),* George M. Wrong, Editor. Toronto, 1939.

Salaman, Redcliffe. *The History and Social Influence of the Potato.* Cambridge, 1949.

Schorger, A.W. *The Passenger Pigeon, Its Natural History and Extinction.* Norman, Oklahoma, 1973.

Scott, Elizabeth. *French Subsistence at Fort Michilimackinac, 1715-1781, The Clergy and the Traders.* Mackinac Island, 1985.

_____. *Such Diet as Befitted his Station as Clerk: The Archaeology of Subsistence and Cultural Diversity at Fort Michilimackinac, 1761-1781* (unpublished thesis). 1991.

Sterling, James. *Letterbook.* William L. Clements Library, University of Michigan, Ann Arbor.

Stone, Lyle. "Archaeology at Fort Michilimackinac," *Mackinac History,* Vol. 2, No. 9. Mackinac Island, 1967.

Stuart, William. *The Potato: Its Culture, Uses, History and Classification.* Philadelphia, 1923.

Sturtevant, William C. *Handbook of North American Indians,* Vol. 15. Washington, D.C., 1978.

Thwaites, Reuben Gold. *The Jesuit Relations and Allied Documents,* Vol. I-LXXIII. New York, 1959.

_____. *New Voyages to North America by the Baron de Lahontan,* Vol. I, 1905.

Trow-Smith, Robert. *A History of British Livestock Husbandry, 1700-1900.* London, 1957.

Tunis, Edwin. *Colonial Living.* New York, 1957.

Voyage to North America de Charlevoix, March of America Facsimile Series, Vol. I. Ann Arbor, 1966.

Warren, William. *History of the Ojibway People.* St. Paul, 1984.

Weatherford, Jack. *Indian Givers, How the Indians of the Americas Transformed the World.* New York, 1988.

_____. *Native Roots, How the Indians Enriched America.* New York, 1991.

Weatherwax, Paul. *Indian Corn in Old America.* New York, 1984.

Welcome Logbook. Alexander Harrow Papers, Burton Collection, Detroit Public Library.

White, Richard. *The Middle Ground.* Cambridge, 1991.

Widder, Keith. "The Persistence of French-Canadian Ways at Mackinac after 1760." (Presentation to French Colonial Historical Society, Mackinac Island, May 18, 1990.)

Williams, Mentor. *Schoolcraft's Indian Legends.* Lansing, 1991.

Wilson, Gilbert. *Buffalo Bird Woman's Garden.* St. Paul, 1987.

Wrong, George M, Editor. *Father Gabriel Sagard: The Long Journey to the Country of the Hurons (1632).* Toronto, 1939.

Wynne, Peter. *Apples: History, Folklore, Horticulture, and Gastronomy.* New York, 1975.

COOKBOOK BIBLIOGRAPHY

Anderson, Jean. *Recipes From America's Restored Villages.* New York, 1975.

Allen, Darina. *The Festive Food of Ireland.* Ireland, 1992.

American Indian Cookbook. Fulton, Michigan, 1974.

Aresty, Esther B. *The Delectable Past.* 1964.

Barer-Stein, Thelma. *You are What You Eat, A Study of Ethnic Food Traditions.* 1979.

Belote, Julianne. *The Compleat American Housewife.* Concord, California, 1974.

Black, Maggie. *Food and Cooking in 19th Century Britain, History and Recipes.* Birmingham, England, 1985.

Boily, Lise, and Jean-Francois Blanchette. *The Bread Ovens of Québec.* Ottawa, 1979.

Breckenridge, Muriel. *The Old Ontario Cookbook.* Canada, 1980.

Bullock, Helen. *The Williamsburg Art of Cookery or Accomplish'd Gentlewoman's Companion.* Williamsburg, 1992.

Buszek, Beatrice. *The Sugar Bush Connection.* Nova Scotia, 1982.

Camp, Charles. *American Foodways, What When Why & How We Eat in America.* Little Rock, 1989.

Carter, Susannah. *The Frugal Colonial Housewife,* edited by Jean McKibbin, reprint of 1742 and 1796, the first published American Cookbook. Garden City, New York, 1976.

Child, Mrs. *The American Frugal Housewife.* Boston, 1833.

Cinqueterre, Berengario delle. *The Renaissance Cookbook, Historical Perspectives Through Cookery.* Crown Point, Indiana, 1975.

Clayton, Bernard Jr. *The Breads of France.* New York, 1978.

Coon, Nelson. *Using Wild and Wayside Plants.* New York, 1980.

Cooper, Jane. *Woodstove Cookery.* Charlotte, Vermont, 1977.

Corbett, Lucy. *French Cooking in Old Detroit.* Detroit, 1951.

Cox, Beverly and Martin Jacobs. *Spirit of the Harvest, North American Indian Cooking.* New York, 1991.

Crump, Nancy Carter. *Hearthside Cooking.* McLean, Virginia, 1986.

Delong, Deanna. *How to Dry Foods.* Tuscon, Arizona, 1979.

Densmore, Frances. *How Indians Use Wild Plants for Food, Medicine & Crafts.* New York, 1974.

Donovan, Mary, Amy Hatrak, Frances Mills, and Elizabeth Shull. *The Thirteen Colonies Cookbook.* New York, 1975.

Dunton, Hope. *From the Hearth.* University College of Cape Breton, 1986.

Ellis, Eleanore. *Northern Cookbook.* Ottawa, 1967.

Farmer, Dennis and Carol. *The King's Bread, 2nd Rising.* Youngstown, New York, 1989.

Farrington, Doris. *Fireside Cooks & Black Kettle Recipes.* Indianapolis, 1976.

"Food History News." Isleboro, Maine.

Franklin, Linda. *America in the Kitchen from Hearth to Cookstove.* Alabama, 1976.

Gardiner, Anne. *Mrs Gardiner's Family Receipts from 1763,* edited by Gail Weesner. Boston, 1938.

Garmey, Jane. *Great British Cooking, A Well-Kept Secret.* 1981.

Glasse, Hannah. *The Art of Cookery Made Plaine and Easy,* (first published 1745). Schenectady, New York, 1994.

Green, Karen and Betty Black. *How to Cook His Goose and Other Wild Game.* New York, 1973.

Grieve, Mrs. M.A. *A Modern Herbal.* New York, 1981.

Hall, Alan. *The Wild Food Trail Guide.* New York, 1973.

Hanson, James A. and Kathryn J. Wilson. *The Buckskinner's Cook Book.* Chadron, Nebraska, 1979.

Homemade Bread, edited by Food Editors of Farm Journal. New York, 1969.

Hopkins, Lynn. *Dutch Oven Secrets.* Utah, 1990.

Hornblower, Malabar. *The Plimoth Plantation New England Cookery Book.* Boston, Mass., 1990.

Kavasch, Barrie. *Native Harvests, Recipes and Botanicals of the American Indian.* New York, 1977.

Kershner, Ruth Bauder. *Irish Cooking.* 1979.

Kidder, Edward. *Receipts of Pastry & Cookery for the Use of His Scholars.* Iowa City, 1993.

Kimball, Marie. *Thomas Jefferson's Cookbook.* Charlottesville, Virginia, 1976.

Krasner, Deborah. *From Celtic Hearths.* New York, 1991.

Kreidberg, Marjorie. *Food on the Frontier.* St. Paul, 1975.

Lowenstein, Eleanor. *Bibliography of American Cookery Books, 1742-1860.* New York, 1972.

Longstreet, Stephen and Ethel. *A Salute to American Cooking.* New York, 1968.

Luecke, Barbara K. *Feeding the Frontier Army, 1775-1865.* Eagan, Minnesota, 1990.

Lund, Duane. *Early Native American Recipes and Remedies.* Cambridge, Maine, 1989.

Martha Washington's Book of Cookery, transcribed by Karen Hess. New York, 1981.

Mitchell, Patricia. *Cooking in the Young Republic, 1780-1850.* Chatham, Virginia, 1992.

Old French Town Cookery. Monroe, Michigan, 1979.

Pastor-Williams, Sara. *The National Trust Book of Traditional Puddings.* 1983.

Perl, Lila. *Hunter's Stew and Hangtown Fry, What Pioneer America Ate and Why.* New York, 1977.

Pitzer, Sara. *Baking with Sourdough,* Bulletin A-50. Powel, Vermont, 1980.

The Presbyterian Cookbook. Dayton, Ohio, 1831.

Ririe, Robert. *Doin Dutch Oven Inside and Out.* 1990.

Ragsdale, John. *Dutch Oven Cooking.* Houston, Texas, 1973.

_____. *Dutch Ovens Chronicled.* Fayetteville, 1991.

Randolph, Mary. *The Virginia Housewife or Methodical Cook.* New York, 1993.

Recipes From the Raleigh Tavern Bake Shop. Williamsburg, Virginia, 1984.

Renfrew, Jane. *Food and Cooking in Prehistoric Britain, History and Recipes.* Birmingham, England, 1985.

Shelton, Ferne, Editor. *Pioneer Cookbook-Campfire and Kitchen Recipes From Early America.* High Point, North Carolina, 1973.

Seventy-Five Receipts, for Pastry, Cakes, and Sweetmeats. By a Lady of Philadelphia. Boston: Munroe and Francis, 1828. Facsimile reprint, Chester, Connecticut.

Simmons, Amelia. *The First American Cookbook, A Facsimile Reprint of American Cookery, 1796.* New York, 1958.

Silitch, Clarissa. *Old Farmer's Almanac Colonial Cookbook.* Dublin, New Hampshire, 1982.

Sloat, Carolyn. *Old Sturbridge Village Cookbook.* Chester, Connecticut, 1988.

Small, Dan and Nancy Fox. *Outdoor Wisconsin Cookbook.* Minocqua, Wisconsin, 1988.

Smith, Eleanor Robertson. *Loyalist Foods in Today's Recipes.* Nova Scotia, 1983.

Stuart, Erling. *Preserving The Catch.* Harrisburg, Pennsylvania, 1982.

Stone, Sally and Martin. *The Brilliant Bean.* New York, 1988.

Tearney, Karalee. "18th and 19th Century Cooking," *The Book of Buckskinning III.* Texarkana, Texas, 1985.

Torgerson, *Food Preservation Before the Mason Jar.* Decatur, Illinois, 1994.

Vennum, Thomas Jr. *Wild Rice and The Ojibway People.* St. Paul, 1988.

Walker, Herb. *Indian Cookery.* Amarillo, Texas, 1977.

Weddon, Willah. *How To Heat and Eat with Woodburning Stoves.* East Lansing, 1980.

Wildlife Chef. Lansing, Michigan, 1981.

Woolf, Cecil and Amelia. *In an Eighteenth Century Kitchen.* Great Britain, 1968.

Wright, Susan and Irene Chalmers. *The Bread Book.* Greensboro, North Carolina, 1972.

GARDENING SOURCES

Newsletter: "Historical Gardener," 1910 North 35th Place, Mount Vernon, Washington, 98273-8981, quarterly newsletter $12.00 per year.

SEED SOURCES

Landis Valley Museum, 2451 Kissel Hill Road, Lancaster, Pennsylvania 17601

Johnny's Selected Seeds, Foss Hill Road, Albion, Maine 04910

Heirloom Seeds, P. O. Box 245, West Elizabeth, Pennsylvania 15088

Old Sturbridge Village, One Old Sturbridge Village Road, Sturbridge, Massachusetts 01566

Select Seeds and Antique Flowers, 180 Stickney Road, Union, Connecticut 06076-4817

Southern Exposure Seed Exchange, P.O. Box 170, Earlyville, Virginia 22936

Native Seeds /SEARCH, 2509 North Campbell Avenue, # 325, Tucson, Arizona 85719

Seed Savers Exchange, Rte # 3, Box 239, Decorah, Iowa 52101

Southmeadow Fruit Garden, Lakeside, Michigan, 49116 (Source for heritage fruit trees)

GLOSSARY

ALE: English term for dark, heavy, bitter beer.

ALUM: double sulfate of ammonium, used in pickling and in dyeing fabrics.

ANDIRON: metal support for firewood, used in a fireplace hearth.

ASHCAKES: cornmeal bread which is wrapped in corn husks and baked in hot ashes.

BAKING POWDER: a powder used as leavening in quick breads and powder cakes. The two main ingredients are baking soda and an acid such as cream of tartar. When moistened, they react to produce carbon dioxide, which raises the dough.

BAKING SODA: sodium bicarbonate, a white powder, that reacts with an acid to produce carbon dioxide, which raises the dough during baking.

BARM: homemade yeast, made from the froth that forms on top of fermenting ale, stored in a stone jar in a cool place such as a root cellar.

BLADDER: animal bladder tied over the mouth of a jar containing preserved foods, used like modern plastic wrap.

BOUILLABAISSE: a French fish stew or chowder.

BRACE: a pair of wild game, such as rabbits or fowl.

BUSTARD: wild goose.

BRINE: a solution of salt and water, for pickling.

CALVES-FOOT JELLY: chilled calves-foot broth, made by boiling calves' feet in water, used as a gelatin.

CASSEROLE: glass, cast iron, or earthenware cooking vessel, used by the early 1700s.

CAUDLE: a hot drink made with wine, sugar, spices, and rice gruel, often given to sick people.

CHAFING DISH: charcoal brazier mounted on a tripod or table top, used to keep food warm and for preserving.

CHOCOLATE: introduced to Europe from Mexico by Cortez in 1528. The pods were picked from the cocoa tree; beans inside were removed and spread out in the sun to ferment and dry. Then the beans were roasted and crushed in a stone trough between stone rollers to a paste that was mixed with water. The Spanish added sugar and mixed it with honey, spices, vanilla, cinnamon, nutmeg, cloves, or aniseed. It was served both hot and cold. Baker's chocolate is an example of period chocolate.

COFFIN: pie dough, a mold of paste for a pie.

COLLARED: cloth was sometimes sewn around meat or fish to keep it fastened tight.

COLLOPS: small pieces or slices of meat. Modern term is scalloped.

CORNED BEEF: meat pickled with salt peter.

CREAM OF TARTAR: potassium bitartrate, white crystal, crushed to a powder, acid in taste and action, made from scrapings of wine vats. Combined with baking soda in baking powder.

CRIMP: to pinch the edge of pastry into a wavy pattern, sealing the edges together.

CRUET: a small glass bottle for holding vinegar or oil at the table, sometimes called a caster.

CULLIS: a strong, clear meat broth or a meat jelly.

DECANT: to pour off gently, without disturbing sediment, as with wine and vinegar.

DEHYDRATION: drying process of removing water from food.

DRAW: to remove the entrails of poultry or game.

DREDGE: to coat with flour.

DRESS: to skin and clean fish or game.

DRIPPINGS: the fat produced by meats as they are spit-roasted, oven-roasted, or pan-fried.

DRY-SALTING: method of salting where dry salt is scattered between layers of fish or meat in a container.

DUTCH OVEN: an iron pot used for baking over coals, has a lid with a lip on which hot coals can be heaped.

FIRKIN: a small wood cask which holds 56 pounds of butter, larger at the bottom than on top. Also a beer measurement (four firkins equals a barrel).

FLIP: a drink with beer, sugar, molasses, dried pumpkin and rum, heated with a hot iron (a fireplace poker called an iron flip dog).

FLUMMERY: dessert of fruit, wine, and cream, sometimes with oatmeal or wheat flour, eggs and spices.

FOOL: a cool, creamy custard.

FORCEMEAT: meat which is finely chopped, highly seasoned and used as a stuffing or garnish; spiced meatballs.

FRESHEN: the process of removing salt from preserved fish or meat by soaking in several baths of fresh water.

GILL: a measurement of ¹/₂ cup, an old English measure equal to ¹/₂ pint.

GOBBETS: small pieces of meat.

GRIDIRON: metal grill or grid, used over coals for grilling fish or meat.

GROG: hot water and rum, served to the British navy in the mid-1700s to prevent scurvy.

HARDTACK: hard biscuit, made with flour and water, no shortening or yeast, also called a sea biscuit.

HAIR SIEVE: a strainer made of horsehair, used to strain soups and sauces, also called a tammy.

HARSHED: hashed or cut into small pieces.

HOE CAKES: cornmeal bread, cooked on a shovel blade over a fire.

HOGSHEAD: large barrel, holds 130-150 gallons of molasses.

HOMINY: hulled corn, corn which has been soaked in lye water to remove the skin, the soft inner kernel of corn.

INDIAN MEAL: cornmeal.

ISINGLASS: a high quality gelatin, formed by melting the swimming bladders of sturgeon.

JACKS: gadget used to turn a spit.

JERKY: meat that is cut thin and dried in the sun; can be smoked.

KETCHUP: a sauce used on meat and fish, made of mushrooms, vegetables, butter, fish, and, in later years, tomatoes.

LEATHER: dried fruit batters, available as early as the 15th century, baked slowly and cut in long strips.

LYE: a strong alkaline solution obtained by soaking wood ashes; used in soapmaking; also added to the water in which dried corn is boiled to soften skin to be removed for hominy.

MACE: a seasoning, the outer cover of nutmeg.

MARINATING: soaking meat or fish in a spice or vinegar solution.

MARROW PUDDING: a pudding made with the marrow or fatty substance from the inside of bones of larger animals, sometimes used as a buttery shortening in cooking.

MIDDLINGS: when flour was ground at home it was sifted and separated. This would be neither the coarsest nor the finest flour.

MINCEMEAT: a way of preserving meat, used as early as the 16th century, made by adding spices and alcohol to the meat.

MORTAR AND PESTLE: bowl and pounding tool used to grind spices, herbs, and sugar.

NEAT'S TONGUE: the tongue of an ox, bull, cow, or heifer.

NUTMEG: the seed of a tree, from the West Indies, which is dried and ground into a flavoring.

PAP SAUCE: bread boiled or softened in milk or water.

PEARLASH: early form of baking powder, ob

tained from wood ashes. Boiling water was poured through the ashes and the resulting lye was strained through coarse linen. This was placed over a hot fire, in a large pot, and evaporated to a black powder. It was then purified by calcination and recrystallized into "pearl-ash." Large quantities were exported from North America to Europe.

PEASE: early name for peas; peasen was the plural form.

PECK: a measure for dry goods, $1/4$ bushel or two gallons.

PEEL: large-handled wooden paddle used to move food in and out of a brick oven.

PEMMICAN: an Indian food made of buffalo or venison meat, dried and compressed into small cakes, containing melted fat and dry berries.

PETTITOES: pig's feet, used as food, also called pig's trotters.

PICKLE: a brine or vinegar solution, used to preserve meat or produce, preserving in an acid solution.

PIPKIN: a wooden bucket with one stave longer than the other to serve as a handle. It was used for dipping from a tub.

PLUCK: the heart, liver, and lungs, used as a food.

PORRINGER: dish made of cast iron, pewter or silver and used to warm and serve small quantities of food.

PORTABLE SOUP: "pocket soup," meat was cooked until it was reduced to a dry bouillon. By adding water later it would be converted back to a broth.

PORTER: a slightly sweet blend of ale and beer.

POSSET: a hot drink consisting of wine, cream, spices, and eggs.

POTTED: cooked meats, fish or cheese, packed in earthenware crocks and sealed with clarified butter.

PUDDING: a mixture of meat, suet, or fruit and seasonings thickened with flour or meal and enclosed in an animal stomach or cloth to be cooked.

PUDDING CLOTH: cloth bag used to boil pudding in, cloth was dipped in hot water, wrung out, floured and filled with batter. It was then boiled in water.

RECEIPT: recipe (from the French *recevoir*, "to get").

REFLECTOR OVEN: tin kitchen, a sheet metal reflector box, open on the side facing the fire, used to reflect heat back on roasting chicken, baked goods, etc.

RENNET: a mass of curdled milk found in the stomach of an unweaned calf, used for the curdling of milk in making cheese.

ROE: eggs found in female fish just before spawning.

ROSE HIPS: seed pod from rose flower, used to make teas to prevent scurvy, provides Vitamin C.

RUST: salt-burned fish or meat, a yellow-red color associated with salted fish that have not been properly stored.

SALAMANDER: a long-handled, flat disk or iron, which was heated in the fire and then quickly passed over a food dish to brown the top.

SALERATUS: an early form of baking soda.

SALLET: salad.

SALT PETER: added to meats to preserve their color, gives meat its red color, prevents it from turning gray.

SAGAMITY: a common meal of the voyageurs, consisting of dried corn meal cooked into a mush with other game or fish added as available.

SCOTCH: to cut shallow, diagonal slashes in skin.

SHRUB: rum or brandy, with sugar and spices, poured over fruit.

SIPPET: small pieces of bread, fried in butter, served in soup or broth, also used to dip gravy.

SMOKING: the method of preserving meat or fish by subjecting them to smoke for an ex tended period of time. The preserving qualities are derived from the particles and vapors deposited on the fish and from the dehydrating effects of the circulating air.

SOLERATUS: see saleratus.

SOURDOUGH: a starter of flour, water (often potato water) and sugar used to allow bread to rise when yeast was not available.

SOUSE: in pickled foods such as herring, the liquid in which the pickling is done.

SPIDER: frying pan with a long handle and three legs to hold it above the coals.

SPIT: an iron spear-pointed rod for holding and turning meat roasting before an open fire.

SPONGE: dough that has been raised and turned into a light, porous mass by the action of the yeast.

SPRUCE BEER: beer brewed in America, used as a common beverage by soldiers and common folk, used as a preventative cure for scurvy.

STARTER: a small portion of dough containing the live micro-organisms that will make vinegar, raise bread dough, or ripen milk for cheese. Vinegar mother, sourdough and raw sour milk are natural starters.

STEW: a dish made by simmering slowly and gently, usually with meat or fish and vegetables.

STOVE: a boiling pot with a tight lid in which to "stove" or sweat meat or game (to steam).

SWEETMEATS: preserved, stewed or brandied fruits (wet) and candied fruit peels (dry).

SYLLABUB: a fancy dessert made of cream, lemon and wine, often served with a garnish. One version states "Fill bowl with wine and place under a cow and then milk the cow into the bowl until a fine froth has formed at the top."

TAMMY: a cloth made from wool or cotton, used as a sieve or strainer.

TEA: a light meal eaten between dinner and supper, also the beverage made from an infusion of water and dried leaves.

TIERCE: a container used to transport wine, equal to 42 gallons.

TINWARE: articles and utensils made of tin plate, which is thin sheet iron or steel coated with tin.

TRAMMEL: an iron gadget with slots, hung on a crane and used to suspend pots over a fire.

TREACLE: British term for molasses.

TREENWARE: wooden plates or spoons, made by hand. Treen was plural form of tree.

TRENCHERS: an early plate, a shallow indentation carved on a flat piece of wood, which kept gravies and sauces from spilling.

TRIVET: three-legged brass or iron stands used to support pans. Coals could be placed under it for baking and it could also be used for serving from a hot pan. Small metal ring trivets were set in Dutch ovens to raise a pie tin off the bottom and allow air to circulate.

TRUSS: to bind, tie, or fasten wings and legs of fowl with string or skewers.

UMBLE PIE: edible organ parts, heart, liver, and entrails, usually of a deer. Servants were often given a pie made of umbles. Eating humble pie meant lowering one's self or deferring to others.

VANILLA: vanilla beans were used as a flavoring for chocolate as early as 1660 in Europe, by splitting the bean and placing in a container with sugar. It was allowed to sit for 2-3 weeks in a cool, dry place to develop flavor. The vanilla sugar was used as flavoring.

VERJUICE: an acid juice of green or unripe grapes, crabapples, or other sour fruit, squeezed and made into a liquor, used in cooking.

WHEY: the watery part of milk left after the removal of the curd.

YEAST: Brewer's yeast or barm was used as a leavening agent. Barm is the froth that forms on top of the fermenting ale or beer and is in liquid form.

INDEX

THE AUTHOR

SALLY EUSTICE has been a craft demonstrator and lead guide at Colonial Michilimackinac each summer since 1989. During the rest of the year she is an elementary school teacher in Cheboygan, Michigan. After graduating from Western Michigan University in 1974 with a BS in Home Economics education, she took additional graduate work at Michigan State University, Central Michigan University and Western Michigan University. She began to teach at a retail fabric shop she opened in 1976. For ten years she taught adults and children to quilt, sew and basketweave. Sally then became an elementary teacher and has taught second, third and fourth grades for the last ten years.

During the summer vacations she can be found at Colonial Michilimackinac hoeing in the garden, spinning wool, dying yarn, or cooking a muskrat stew in the fireplace. Sally says, "This fort is a place where all my hobbies and interests come together. Here, visitors are interested in learning about our pioneer ancestors' lives. We can teach by doing and let them experience a taste of living history. Being able to teach here, using all the hands-on displays and props, is a very effective method of teaching."